Aegean Quest

By the same author

NOVELS

The House of Whipplestaff (Hodder & Stoughton)
Merlin Hold (Jarrolds)
A Stranger in These Parts (Skeffington)
The General in Retreat (Centaur Press)

PLAYS

X.O.3
Knight Errant (filmed as The Girl in the Night)
Blood Royal
He Loves Me Not
Inactive Service

CHILDREN'S PLAYS

Mariposa Bung (Samuel French)
The Seventeenth Highwayman (Samuel French & Harrap)
The Deuce (Samuel French)

ANTHOLOGY

Benjamin Disraeli (Falcon Press)

TRAVEL

In Crusader Greece (Centaur Press)

AEGEAN QUEST

A Search for Venetian Greece

By

Eric Forbes-Boyd

with photographs by
Aileen Forbes-Boyd

NEW YORK
W. W. NORTON & CO. INC.

DF
901
C9F65
1970 b

Printed in Great Britain

First published 1970

SBN: 393 08604 6

Contents

List of Illustrations

(*Between pages 66 and 67*)

(*Between pages 130 and 131*)

Acknowledgments

For the historical facts in this book I have drawn mainly upon William Miller's The Latins in the Levant, and his Essays on the Latin Orient; I have also made use of Jean Longnon's L'Empire Latin de Constantinople, Finlay's Medieval Greece and Trebizond, his Greece under Othoman and Venetian Domination and his History of the Greek Revolution; and lastly I must mention Jean Baelen's Mykonos: Chronique d'une île de l'Egée. Other writings to which I have referred, and the sources of all quotations, have been acknowledged in the Notes.

Passages in chapters four, five, eight and ten, and several paragraphs elsewhere in the book have appeared in articles of mine published in The Christian Science Monitor, and I am grateful to the editor of this newspaper for permission to use them.

I am much indebted to the library of The Society for the Promotion of Hellenic Studies; and finally I should like to express my thanks to Miss Nancy Ferguson of the Ulster Museum for making enlargements of many of my wife's photographs.

For those who may care to have an outline of the period, I have added, at the end of the book, a table of the main events.

As regards the spelling of names, I have merely used in each case the version that seemed best known.

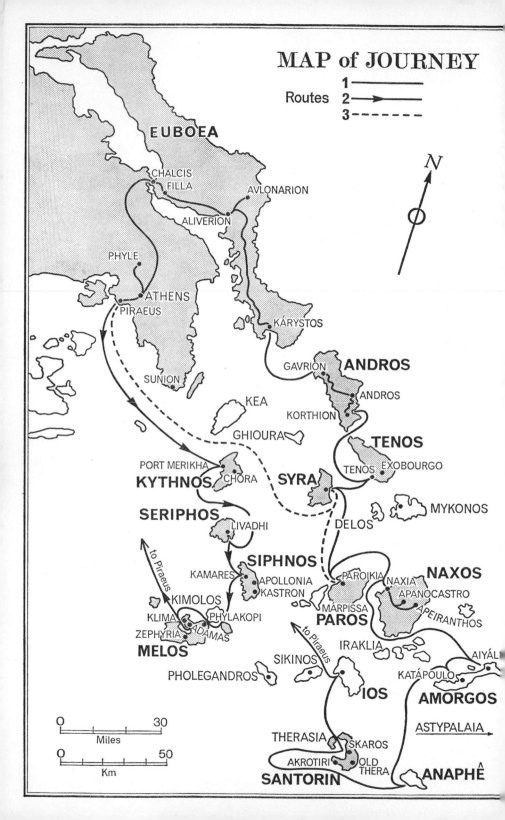

Chapter One

ATHENS: The Golden Age
EUBOEA: Siege of Negroponte

LEAVING London for Athens, we had a rather burdened sense of the amount we had to do within our allotted time of four weeks. Aileen looked back regretfully to the spacious days of the Grand Tour, when one took a couple of years to make the round of Europe, and, as likely as not, travelled in the family coach with a bevy of servants in attendance. In fact Byron, according to Medwin, took with him 'seven servants, five carriages, nine horses, a monkey, a bull-dog and a mastiff, two cats, three pea-fowls and some hens'![1] But the only member of a Grand Tour retinue for whom I had any wish was a Greek-speaking courier: he would have saved us no end of bother, as will be seen.

However, a few hours in Athens did much to counteract the feeling of Time treading on our heels: for the racketty, bustling city has a way of propagating a happy-go-lucky attitude in its people, and even in its visitors. In our case it may have been no more than the contrast with well-drilled London, where the police stroll about carefree and majestic, but the people wear a harassed look; while in Athens it is the people who are carefree, and the police who look harassed. Athens is indeed far from well-drilled; there is even a plainly held sentiment in her crowds that pedestrians are of greater importance than the traffic, a notion that would be regarded as thoroughly subversive in London.

Anyway, whatever had got into us, we spent the first day idling.

We went of course to the Acropolis; since, however many times you have seen it, it is impossible not to visit the Acropolis when you come to Athens; for it is on this rock that all one's visions of ancient Greece are ultimately founded, and it never fails to induce a thrill of excitement in me. Yet I confess this is not altogether due to its architectural beauty. Greek architecture has been so copied and vulgarized in the modern world that at every turn in the cities of today one encounters Ionic or Corinthian columns, or some tasteless adaptation of a classic portico; and I find it difficult when I meet the genuine article not to see in it a twice-told tale.

I am far from sharing the reactions of Bernard Shaw, who wrote to Ellen Terry complaining of the horrors of travelling among the islands, and added: 'However, I am at least quit of Athens, with its stupid classic Acropolis and smashed pillars'.[2] For the Parthenon, with those exquisite proportions that are a miracle of contrivance, does assert itself, and open a vista of beauty through the forest of imitation columns that distract the mind's eye; but it does not make me catch my breath—and still less am I moved by the Erechtheum, which, apart from that heavy caryatid porch, is for me a largely meaningless jumble of walls.

Much greater is the impact of the natural features of this astonishing rock, standing up in such majestic and incredible isolation in the midst of the plain that one tends to imagine it as the result of some Olympian intervention, as the spring of Hippocrene was created by the hoof-stroke of Pegasus. But what counts most with me, as, I imagine, with many people, is simply the evocative power of the scene, its effortless projection of the past, a phenomenon that I find more rewarding than ravaged beauty. Peculiarly rewarding in this case. For the Greek story reaches us largely as the creation of the great writers of the ancient world, and their very artistic ability has the effect of lending a literary, slightly unreal glamour to the people and events of which they write, of raising them almost to the level of legend or myth. The Socrates of Plato and

2

Xenophon, even the Pericles of Thucydides, come to seem as much a part of an heroic, even fabulous age, as the Agamemnon of Homer or of Aeschylus; and the great doings on the plain of Marathon seem as much larger than life in the epic of Herodotus as those on the plain of Troy in the Iliad. Hence there is an especially satisfying thrill when it is the golden, improbable, miraculous age of classic Greece that is not merely evoked as a memory, but brought down to earth by some tangible survival. It is for that I return as often as I can to the Acropolis.

The next day we took a taxi to Phyle, the fifth-century fort on the northern boundary of Attica in the folds of Mount Parnes. The fort is still impressive, and so, too, is the effect of this wild frontier with its clustering, inhospitable hills, erupting into great red and grey cliffs, or covered with scrub and green patches of the thorny kermes oak. Seen from Phyle, as one looks south, it is a knotted tangle of ridges and ravines, marked only here and there by what appears to be a dried watercourse, but may be a track, or is perhaps both—if there be any truth in Edmond About's jibe that 'the Greeks dispense with making a road whenever water has been willing to take on the job'. Here, on the north-east, is the bastion of naked rock known as Mount Pagania. This, according to Sir James Frazer, is the ancient Mount Harma, which in thundery weather was kept under close observation by the augurs at Athens, who watched for the moment when they should see lightning strike its summit—the signal for them to offer sacrifice at Delphi.[3]

But Phyle was really not in our plan, since our purpose in coming to Greece was to see such relics as were left of those picturesque Latin states set up by the Crusaders at the beginning of the thirteenth century in the islands of the Aegean.

In the year 1204 the host that had embarked on the Fourth Crusade to rescue Jerusalem from the Infidel startled Europe by attacking instead the Christian city of Constantinople, the capital of the Greek Byzantine Empire. When this had been stormed, and ruthlessly sacked, and the Greek Emperor had fled, the Crusaders elected their own leader, Baldwin, Count of Flanders, as Emperor, and set out to take possession of the lands that had belonged to the Empire.

In the Morea they founded the Principality of Achaia; they united Attica and Boeotia into a state that later became known as the Duchy of Athens; and they created a short-lived Kingdom of Salonica. In addition they set up various smaller fiefs, such as the County of Salona at the foot of Parnassus, the Marquisate of Boudonitza at Thermopylae, and the three baronies of Euboea.

But besides these there were the lands that fell to Venice— and the Lion of St Mark's share of the spoils was appropriately large. For Venice had been the instigator of the whole coup, and, under the gallant leadership of her Doge, Enrico Dandolo, who was ninety years old and blind, she had borne much of the brunt of the fighting; moreover the Crusaders owed her money. Not only did she receive large tracts in the Peloponnesus and in Epirus, but in addition she obtained the best harbours in the Levant, and most of the islands in the Aegean.

These islands, however, were occupied by Greeks, and would have to be conquered; but in view of her other commitments, the Republic felt that this would be too great a strain for her. She therefore conceived the plan of offering the islands as a prize to any of her citizens who cared to undertake, with their own resources, the task of reducing them: if they succeeded, it would cost her nothing, while the resulting colonies could be trusted to live on friendly terms with her, since they would be certain to need her protection.

There was plenty of enterprise and courage in thirteenth-century Venice, and a nephew of the heroic old Dandolo immediately took advantage of the Republic's offer. He was Marco Sanudo, a man of some wealth, who had followed his uncle to Constantinople, where he had distinguished himself as a soldier and a diplomat, and had been made a judge in one of the courts set up by the conquerors. He resigned his seat on the bench, gathered a few companions, and a small force of mercenaries, equipped eight galleys, and sailed off to the Aegean, where, having captured a number of islands, he founded the Duchy of Naxos, which was to last for three hundred and fifty-nine years.

We had been fascinated by this interlude in Greek history, when Greece became the home of chivalry, and knighthood flowered on all the classic sites from Thebes and Athens to Sparta and the Islands. It seemed to us that the chronicles of these Frankish states were rich in characters, in spectacular incident, and Websterian tragedy; and we had finally become so enthusiastic as to make a tour of the Frankish castles of the Morea.* Now we were bound for Euboea, and for the Aegean where the Sanudi, the Ghisi, the Barozzi, the Gozzadini, the da Corogna, and others, had ruled their petty states, and enacted that unique and fantastic drama of the Lords of the Isles.

The following morning we caught a bus for Chalcis on Euboea. We had some difficulty in finding the bus, for the Greeks are seldom well up in local knowledge—a fact of which we became acutely aware on our travels. The taxi-driver, the day before, had never heard of Phyle although it was only fourteen miles from Athens. But historic monuments seem to mean little to them, unless it be a monastery, or something connected with the War of Independence. The only history they care to remember is their latest chapter as a free people, and this of course is understandable: they appreciate their classical ruins, as a tourist attraction, but in general they do not take much interest in them, although they will maintain stoutly their descent from the Greeks of the ancient world.

Less understandable is their equal vagueness in other departments of local knowledge. Ask in a Barsetshire village when and where the next bus goes to Plumstead Episcopi, and—man, woman and child—the whole population has the answer pat; but in a Greek village you may get, as we once did, three

* See In Crusader Greece, by the author (Centaur Press, 1964).

different times for a bus, and two different departure points. One has the impression that buses are flighty creatures, here today and gone tomorrow, but that beyond this even the most travel-wise inhabitant is on delicate ground, and imprudent to commit himself. A most unjust slur on Greek buses, which in the main run well to time.

The road, accompanying the railway, runs through the gap between Parnes and Pentelicus; and anyone with the idea that Attica is a barren, stony land would be surprised at the fertility of this plain, where we saw vineyards, lemon trees, acres of potatoes, pasture with sheep grazing, and wide-stretching cornfields. The last were of course in stubble, with a few withered stalks of asphodel, which is sometimes used to mark boundaries, drooping here and there over the field like the pennons of an army that had fled.

Shortly before it reaches Chalcis, the road winds up to a height, and offers a fine view across the Euripus and the roofs of the town to Euboea, to the blue and sepia backcloth of rolling hills and valleys that culminate in the Dhirfis range on the horizon. This was the view that Sultan Mohammed II paused to admire, when he came on a friendly visit to Negroponte—twelve years before he led his armies to attack it.

Euboea, 'the eyebrow of the Latins' as the Byzantine historian called it, was the first of our islands, and we looked at it with expectancy. The sailors of King Alcinous in the *Odyssey* held it to be 'the furthest of lands',[4] and even today, apart from Chalcis, it is rather off the track of tourists; but it had much to offer us. For those hills had seen the brilliant exploits of the renegade, Licario; the campaigning of William de Villehardouin; the spectacular rise of Bonifacio da Verona, the favourite who made good; and the onset of those ruthless fighters, the Catalan Grand Company. While over the ground immediately before us had been fought that gallant and tragic passage of arms, the defence of Negroponte by the Venetians against the Turks under Mohammed II—one of the most celebrated episodes in the war that was waged, off and on,

6

between these two powers for some four hundred years.

The old bridge across the narrows, which had given Chalcis its medieval name of Negroponte—derived from 'Egripoponte', and meaning bridge over the Euripus—had had a Venetian tower in the middle, on an artificial island that divided the channel into two. The tower was destroyed in 1896; the smaller, western, channel was then filled in, and covered by a permanent causeway leading to a swing bridge over the second, and wider channel. This is the present bridge.

To our left, on the near bank of the Euripus, rose the hill on which stands the seventeenth-century Turkish fort of Karababa, commanding the town and the strait. Chalcis itself was posing for us in the only position in which it exhibits any charm; for, so far as looks go, the town is a mere façade, with nothing to recommend it but a pleasant waterfront, of the purely conventional kind—small, white hotels, cafés with awnings, caiques at the quay, and along the promenade, plantations of oleanders. There is not a relic anywhere to suggest this as the scene of a bloody and desperate fight, of massacre and cruelties unspeakable. Even Karababa, confronting Chalcis across the water, has a most unmartial air, since in its later years it has been decorated with a belfry; but indeed the fort was built two centuries after the siege of Negroponte, and has played little part in the stirring events here.

The Frankish story begins in the year 1205, when Euboea was conquered by Jacques d'Avesnes, a Fleming in the army that Boniface de Montferrat led into Greece after the Crusaders' conquest of Constantinople. When d'Avesnes died, Boniface divided the island among three gentlemen of Verona; and this division into three baronies, although it was often modified by circumstances, remained the basic political pattern of the island during its occupation by the Latins.

At first the allegiance of these barons, or 'triarchs', lay rather doubtfully between Venice and the de Villehardouin Princes of Achaia; but as time went on Venice became in fact paramount. The Republic had appointed a Bailie at Negroponte to govern its settlements, and his authority gradually spread over the whole island: when there was a dispute between the barons, it was to him they appealed; he intervened and arbitrated, having behind him the power of the Venetian navy; and from the capital, which was shared by the triarchs, and was the political and social centre of the island, he kept a watchful eye on the proceedings of them all.

In 1259 William de Villehardouin, Prince of Achaia, was captured by the Byzantine Greeks at the battle of Pelagonia, and one result of this was to give Euboea a rare spell of quiet. Indeed, Sanudo, the Venetian historian, says that it fell 'into a state so peaceful that the enemy of the human race would have had it in envy'.[5] Its inhabitants, however, were hardly so peacefully minded: castles had risen all over the island, and from these the barons would launch raids upon the sea, and pursue remunerative careers as pirates.

At this time the Aegean was an area of perpetual conflict. The Greeks of Nicaea were forever seeking to drive out the Franks, to regain Constantinople and the former Byzantine Empire; the Venetians and Genoese were deadly trade rivals, between whom there was always either a cold war or open hostilities; the fleets of the Seljuk emirs swarmed out from the coast of Asia Minor, plundering and enslaving all unbelievers, whether they were Greeks or Franks—and such fleets were but a part of the vast horde of pirates that quartered these troubled waters in search of prey.

So numerous, formidable and ruthless were the pirates that some defence against, or refuge from, them was indispensable to existence in the islands. Every nation round the Mediterranean seaboard was represented among them; and the authority and influence of some of the captains were immense. As in the days of Odysseus, piracy was a not unrespectable profession; and even the Dukes of Athens thought it no shame to do a little in a quiet way. Pirates of less illustrious status might yet, if they had a reputation for seamanship and hard fighting, be transformed overnight into the accredited commanders of

8

some state or sovereign—as happened in the case of the notorious corsair, John de lo Cavo, who became Lord High Admiral to the Greek Emperor. Or there was the later and more famous case of Khaireddin Barbarossa and the Grand Turk.

The two brothers known as Barbarossa, from their red beards, were descended from Albanian and Greek parents who were Christians. Both brothers fought their way in spectacular fashion to the position of noted pirates; but the elder was killed comparatively early, while the younger, Khaireddin, in a career that was full of dramatic reversals of fortune, became eventually so commanding a figure that none of the nations round the Mediterranean dared to disregard him. As savage a ruffian as history can show, he was nevertheless perhaps the greatest seaman of his day, with no-one to rival him unless it were Andrea Doria of Genoa; so that it was not without good reason that Suleiman the Magnificent, in 1533, made Barbarossa Captain-General of his fleet.

In the last half of the thirteenth century, the Byzantine Greeks, who had now retaken Constantinople, captured most of Euboea, but the Latins soon recovered it; and then, in 1311, came the conquest of the Duchy of Athens by the Catalans, and a new foe menaced Euboea.

In the end Venice contrived to keep the Catalans out of Euboea, except for a couple of castles that came to their vicar-general by inheritance; but she was not so successful against the Turks. In the twenty years preceding 1470, these were everywhere victorious: they took Constantinople and the Morea from the Greeks, who had previously destroyed the Frankish Principality of Achaia; they absorbed the Duchy of Athens, and all the smaller Frankish domains in central Greece. Thus Venice was left alone to face them in defence of her possessions in the Morea and the islands. There were three years of warfare not very favourable to the Republic; and then the climax came in 1470 at Negroponte.

As we wound down the hill to the swing bridge, we had a good view of the arena. On our right, to the south of the town, was Bourkos bay where, on 15th June, 1470, the Turkish fleet, with an army aboard, cast anchor. Shortly afterwards, the Sultan led in another army from Thebes; a bridge of boats was thrown across to the island, south of the narrows, the army passed over, and extended its lines east of the town. On our left, where Karababa now stands, a battery was raised, and a second bridge was drawn across north of the narrows; thus the town was surrounded on all sides but the north, while the whole circumference, and the adjacent country, were swept continually by the Turkish cavalry.

Estimates of the Turkish army vary from 120,000 to 300,000; the town, which contained 2,500 inhabitants and many fugitives, had in addition to its Venetian garrison, 700 men from Crete, and 500 soldiers under a captain from Dalmatia named Tommaso. In command was the Venetian Bailie, Paolo Erizzo, who, although he had completed his term of office, elected to remain.

After a not very successful bombardment from twenty-one cannon, the Turks, having filled the moat with fascines, attacked; but the garrison set fire to the fascines, and the assault was driven back with great loss. Four days later, another attack was repulsed with even heavier loss.

Meanwhile, the castle of La Cuppa, some miles away near Avlonarion, had been betrayed to the Turks, and those within were brought to Negroponte, and butchered before the walls as a warning to the garrison. A similar attempt was now made to obtain Negroponte by treachery.

But the plot was revealed. A man was found missing; an old Greek woman had a story to tell of the mistress of Tommaso; the threat of torture induced another conspirator to speak; and finally, three arrows were found, attached to which were messages that left no doubt of Tommaso's guilt.

The traitor, hearing that his accomplices had been arrested, determined to brazen it out; and with a large following, he rode down to the town square to demand satisfaction from the Bailie. But he found the square lined with Erizzo's men. The

Bailie, however, playing the friendly innocent, managed to quiet the traitor's alarm. Tommaso dismounted, and followed the Bailie into his residence—and the instant he was across the threshold, he was run through by the sword of every man within who could reach him.

A third assault on the town, into which the Sultan was lured under the impression that Tommaso was still co-operating with him, proved the most expensive of all to the Turks. Four days later, when the siege had been in progress for seventeen days, a fourth attack was begun——when the Turks beheld a Venetian fleet, under Niccolò da Canale, sailing to the rescue down the channel north of the Euripus.

The Sultan was in despair; and had Canale attacked and destroyed the two bridges of boats, which would have been comparatively easy, it seems fairly certain that Negroponte might have been saved. But the Admiral was too cowardly, or, more likely, too cautious; he declared he must wait until the rest of the fleet came up—and he cast anchor six miles north of the town. At this, the Sultan took heart again, and worked like a demon to retrieve the situation. He made preparations in case Canale should land; he filled the moat again, this time with dead bodies that stank horribly, as well as with casks and fascines; and, on the following morning, he mounted a fifth assault.

The garrison signalled for help to the fleet, but Canale never moved; and after desperate fighting, the Turks succeeded in carrying an outwork on the south, and then the main walls. Still the fighting went on from street to street in the town. The last stand was made in the square. From this the Bailie escaped, and, with a number of women and children, managed to reach the tower in the middle of the bridge over the Euripus.

The fleet made a demonstration, but retired; and after that there was no choice but surrender.

Then took place one of those scenes of appalling ferocity for which the Turk was notorious above all nations in the medieval world. There was a general massacre, in which the

Sultan himself did not disdain to ride through the streets hunting for any fugitives who might have escaped. The gallant Erizzo was put to death in a peculiarly horrible manner; and it was said that no male over the age of eight was left alive.[6]

Canale was tried at Venice, and banished from the state.

It is sad to reflect that as late as the last decade of the nine-teenth century the Venetian fortifications of the town were still to be seen. Writing in the 'eighties, Major Gambier Parry says:

'The appearance of Chalcis is most striking. . . . Viewed from the port, Chalcis seems to be entirely surrounded by an elaborate system of fortifications, above which the dome of a mosque, a ruined minaret, or the dark red roofs of a few houses are alone visible. The walls which encircle the place are of a rich yellow colour, and their ruined battlements, flanking towers, intricate gateways, and generally compli-cated involution give them a most picturesque appearance.'[7]

It is a description that leaves one full of regrets for the vanish-ing of an evocative scene, and of a worthy memorial to the brave men who fought here.

The famous Euripus current is reputed to change up to fourteen times in the twenty-four hours, and everyone has heard the quite unfounded legend that Aristotle committed suicide because he could not solve the problem of this chang-ing current; so far as I know, it is still a mystery, but our modern scientists fortunately do not take it to heart. It never seemed a friendly water to me; white horses, hinting at inward torments, were nearly always showing, and I wouldn't have cared to bathe in it, particularly after I had seen a great squad-ron of jellyfish heaving by on the current, dark, sinister blobs like a batch of miniature floating mines.

There is not much to see in Chalcis. Apart from the cannon balls used in the great siege, which are piled in the square, almost the only relic of Frankish days is the church of Ayia Paraskeví, a Byzantine basilica converted by the Latins into a Gothic cathedral. The outside, with its much restored Italianate tower, is not very impressive; but in this land of domes and drums, the Gothic interior makes an immediate appeal to English people, with its two rows of pointed arches, and the fine rib-vaulting of the chapels that terminate the aisles; worth a long look, too, is the boss in the south chapel on which is carved the strikingly animated head of a roaring leopard.

That evening we wandered along the front in search of an eating place. Some of these are of the taverna class, with charcoal braziers on the pavement before them, where the meat or fish is grilled; but we chose a more conventional restaurant, in which, as so often in Greece, the food was indifferent, but the staff attentive and genial. We were invited into the kitchen to select our dishes—much the most satisfactory way of ordering; but somehow the promise of the stove with its bubbling pots is rarely fulfilled, for Greek food has the secret of cooling as Greek fire had of burning, and no matter how short the distance from the kitchen, it comes to table, more often than not, lukewarm. A state I find as revolting in food as St John found it in other matters, and I could cheerfully echo his: 'I will spew thee out of my mouth'! It is partly mismanagement, and partly, I think, eccentricity, for there are things, such as French beans, that appear to be served cold on purpose.

It was at this restaurant that we encountered the enigma of the nut-pedlar. He was a well-dressed fellow who spent the time between his rounds at one of the tables on the pavement; when he judged the moment was right, he would get to his feet, pick up his large basket, and circulate among the customers in the restaurant, pausing here and there to chat, and offer his little bags of pistachio nuts. A good-humoured character, with jovial manners, he was certainly popular with the habitués—but very rarely did we see him make a sale. It didn't appear to depress him. He would drift back to his seat, and relax contentedly until the time came for another round. How did he make a living? And even a good living, if one might judge from his clothes.

I understand that the solution lies in the fact that the nut-pedlar is really carrying on a surreptitious gambling game with the customers; he has some loose nuts at the bottom of his basket, picks up a handful of these, and the customer bets on the number being odd or even. We did not know this at the time, nor did we get any hint of it; but looking back, I think it was possible that we may have been watching a sporting event.[8]

After it was dark, we strolled into the hinterland of the town, and found it, behind that conventional façade, ill-lit and depressing, with shops that lurked furtively in the narrow streets, their windows only faintly illuminated, as though they shunned attention, which is unnatural behaviour in shops. At the end of one of these streets, we came upon a woman begging. She sat on the pavement, her legs stretched out parallel to, and almost on, the kerb; swathed from head to foot in black, she had a black scarf wound over her head, and drawn, like a yashmak, across the lower part of her face, and in the gloom of the street not even her eyes could be seen. She never moved. Her head was bowed. One hand protruded from her wrappings, palm upward. I put a few drachmae in the hand. There was no response, only the hand slowly withdrew into those mummy folds, and slowly returned without the money, palm upward.

The next night I went through the ritual again. Nobody spoke to her; nor did I see anyone else drop money into that hand—which remained upturned without a tremble, neither importunate, nor, so far as could be deduced, grateful for alms, nor resentful at the lack of them, but simply extended indifferently to Fate.

Chapter Two

EUBOEA

Licario the Renegade

W E went across on the afternoon of our arrival to inspect the fort of Karababa on its hill overlooking the Euripus.
It is hardly a powerful stronghold. The Turks built it, in the 1680s, and they, magnificent fighters though they have always been, were seldom much use at designing and constructing fortifications, and Karababa, with its belfry and peculiar battlements, has an element of the absurd, which becomes even more evident when one reflects that this is not a medieval castle, but a fortress designed for artillery warfare.

The ground plan is triangular, with a short base parallel to the Euripus, and an apex pointing west. The strong point of the fort, which housed the most important of its batteries, is the polygonal bastion at the northern end of the base. This commands the Euripus, the bridge, and the bays to north and south of the narrows; and it was mainly to achieve this zone of fire that the fort was built. The ground within the enclosure slopes up for a distance of about 500 feet to the apex, which is marked by a seven-sided bastion, commanding the road from Thebes.

We went through the main gate, at the south-east corner, into the enclosure, and were at once struck with amazement by the rococo battlements, which extend along the whole of the north curtain, and portions of the south. Scallop-shaped and quite unpractical, being too high to allow of fire between their rounded tops, for which reason they had to be loopholed, they look like part of a stage set for the Duke of Plaza-Toro's castle. But if they do not inspire respect, they at any rate make a lighthearted appeal as of a kind of fortress folly, designed not so much for defence as for a martial decoration!

It was not taken too seriously, either, by Morosini, the great Venetian commander, who, at the head of a mixed army, composed mainly of Venetians and Germans, sat down to besiege Negroponte in 1688. He had already in a series of brilliant campaigns conquered the whole of the Morea from the Turks; and the latter, anticipating he would make an attempt on Negroponte, had built Karababa in haste as an additional defence. But Morosini when he came, hearing that Karababa had no proper water supply, determined to ignore it —contrary to the advice of his second-in-command, Count Königsmarck. The latter proved to be right, for the presence of Karababa enabled reinforcements to reach the town.

Sickness and battle casualties greatly reduced the Venetian army, and by the end of three months its numbers did not much exceed those of the garrison. Nevertheless, Morosini determined to make one desperate attempt to carry the town by storm. After violent fighting, he was driven off with the loss of a thousand men; upon which he was left with no alternative but to raise the siege.[1]

One of the leaders in this attack was Königsmarck's nephew, Carl, who forms a link of a kind with England. 'A beauty, a dandy, a warrior, a rascal of more than ordinary mark', as Thackeray describes him,[2] he had eloped with the wife of an English peer in Venice, and taken her on active service disguised as his page. Later, in England, he had fallen violently in love with an heiress, Lady Elizabeth Ogley, who became the wife of Thomas Thynne; and when Thynne was murdered, Carl was accused of the crime. He was tried, and acquitted, but had to leave England in a hurry—to die eventually of fever here at Negroponte.

In April 1941 Karababa looked on again at some spectacular

action, when the Germans dive-bombed the harbour at Chalcis, sinking many ships; simultaneously, a German flanking movement through Euboea took Chalcis, and crossed the Euripus to the mainland in pursuit of the British army.

We walked up the enclosure to the apex bastion where a flight of steps led down to two concentric galleries beneath the upper gun platform. From the platform we had a good view over the castle: the ground about it fell only moderately steeply, and on the slopes, tall, shapely young cypresses were scattered like a wave of skirmishers leading the advance of Birnam Wood, or an attack of the triffids.

There were other, and genuinely hostile vegetables present; for as we walked back, we came on that peculiar plant, the squirting cucumber, which, if you touch it, fires off its seed at you, accompanied by an acrid poisonous juice. This occurs only at the season when its seed is ripe, and it is reliably reported to achieve then a range of twenty feet; but neither of us has ever witnessed so fine a shoot!

In the nineteenth century Euboea was a favourite haunt of bandits; and quite a stir was caused when, on Christmas Day 1855, they kidnapped Mlle Boudouris, the young daughter of a wealthy Greek senator, from her father's house on the out-skirts of Chalcis. They plundered the house, threatened the mother with torture, and when they were interrupted, carried off Mlle Boudouris, together with her small brother and her brother-in-law. Two months later, after being dragged through the mountains as far as Helicon and Parnassus, the captives were ransomed for two thousand pounds. Not only did this affair terminate more happily than some others at the time; but it appears not to have been such an alarming ordeal for the lady as it sounds. For about four years later, Sir Thomas Wyse, the British ambassador to Greece, met her.

'She liked it very well [he writes] and was not the least afraid. Of what should she be afraid? She lived well, was healthy in consequence, had always psito, or roast meat, and the clearest water. She . . . seemed to think the whole very natural and rather good fun.'[3]

We learn that when her shoes wore out, the bandits bought her new ones from the nearest town; and a final gesture, worthy of Le Roi des Montagnes himself, is recorded by Sir Thomas's niece: 'Daveli, the chief, had the gallantry, too, to bestow, as a parting present, on Mlle Boudouris, the ornaments and jewels which he had stolen from her mother!'[4] It is true, however, that he added the keep of his prisoners to the bill for ransom, which strikes one as niggling, and not quite in the grand manner.

We had decided to visit next the castle at Alivérion, which lies on the coast of Euboea, about twenty-five miles south of Chalcis; and we went along to book tickets on the bus for the following day. Making inquiries about times of buses from the man in the office, I was getting on competently, if rather slowly, until a helpful tourist policeman came up to lend a hand, and had us tangled in no time. His English was as poor as my Greek, but he, unfortunately, was much more confident; not aware of this at first, I thankfully had recourse to English, upon which he immediately got me wrong, and misled the official at great length.

It took time and toil to get them off the scent of this red herring. I did my best to do it without hurting anyone's feelings, but, as I have so often found, it is difficult to be tactful with little more equipment than nods and becks and wreathed smiles.

These tourist policemen are invariably charming and courteous, with an overwhelming desire to help; but Aileen sighs whenever one bears down upon us, and although I tell her this is due to her Irish blood and its antipathy to a 'polisman', I must confess they can be a trial. For it is practically a point of honour for them to understand you—and it is so much more exhausting to talk to the bluffers than to the blank.

The next morning we caught the bus for Alivérion at 9.30.

Sitting next to us, across the gangway, was an Americano—
that is, a Greek who has spent some years in the United States,
and speaks English. Luckily for us, one comes across many of
these as one travels in Greece, and we owe an immense
amount to their kindness. It is another happy circumstance,
from our point of view, that they are nearly always to be distinguished by a panama hat, which appears to confer a kind
of cosmopolitan cachet. He began to talk to us; for an Americano is always delighted to air his English.

Usually, on such occasions there are certain matters upon
which a Greek likes to make a preliminary check: Where do
we come from? Is this my wife? How long have we been
married? How many children have we? At which point,
having learnt that we have been married for over twenty years
and have no children, he shakes his head commiseratingly,
and allows a decent pause to cover what he imagines must be
our embarrassment at such a humiliating situation. Then,
enlightened upon these vital matters, he politely reciprocates
with a brief sketch of his own happy domestic position and
abundant offspring. It is only after this ritual that one can get
down to business.

In this case, however, our man turned out to be indeed a
cosmopolitan, and he at once responded to my tentative
inquiries about castles. Nothing is more difficult than to
obtain beforehand reliable information about the Greek
castles, unless they be as celebrated as Khlemoutsi or the
Palamedi. Generally speaking no-one knows, or cares, about
them; and it is not until you are within a stone's throw of your
castle that you can be sure of learning even its exact position.
I was delighted, therefore, when he showed some knowledge
of the castles in the neighbourhood.

Yes, there was a castle at Filla, which we should be able to
see in the distance; another at Alivérion, and yet another
beyond this at Avlonarion.

I pricked up my ears: it seemed to me that the last might
well be the famous La Cuppa, which has already been men-

tioned in connection with the siege of Negroponte. I knew it lay close to Avlonarion. Where, I asked, was it precisely? Right in the middle of the town, was the reply. I was surprised. He appealed to the bus generally: Was not the castro at Avlonarion in the town? With one voice the bus bore him out. Undoubtedly it was.

Naturally, the affair did not end there. Visitors are rare in Euboea, and from the beginning we had aroused the curiosity of the bus. Now, having been put au courant with our affairs, the bus made haste to help, and took up the subject of castros with enthusiasm: suggestions were made, statements were argued; and in a moment there was a tumult of debate, conducted at the high pitch necessary to dominate the melancholy *bouzouki* wailings of the driver's radio.

After leaving Chalcis and winding along the shore at the foot of the hills, the road enters the far-famed Lelantine plain, where there are eucalyptus trees and an abundance of olives. Fifty years ago, according to our Americano, there were no olive trees here, but the advent of electric power, enabling water to be pumped up for irrigation, led to many trees being planted. Presently we reached Nea Psara, which is the ancient Eritrea—the unsuccessful contender in the famous Lelantine war—where there are still the ruins of a theatre, a bath and a gymnasium. Not far beyond is the tiny, unexpected resort of Amárinthos, where a handful of villas on the shore, a café and a few coloured awnings, make a perky attempt at gay sophistication in the wilderness—and manage, as Greek villages nearly always manage, to look charming and peaceful if a trifle down-at-heel.

Meanwhile, the debate on what we ought to do had continued, and the general opinion seemed to be that we should proceed to Avlonarion. Aileen and I conferred hastily. The distance from Alivérion to Avlonarion, appropriately reminiscent of the more celebrated relation of Wimbledon to Wombledon, was fourteen kilometres or thereabouts, and we determined to go on.

The bus stop at Avlonarion is about half a mile from the village, on the main road where there is a café, and a house or two. Here we got out; and the whole bus, passengers and crew, followed us, and, grouped before the café, gave us a great send-off.

'*Adió! Adió! Sto kaló!*'—Goodbye! Goodbye! (Go) to good!—they cried, waving vigorously. No doubt they had got down to stretch their legs, or to have a drink; but it was warm-hearted and friendly all the same, and we were touched. Though we could not escape an uneasy feeling that they looked upon us as venturing into a wild and unexplored hinterland in which anything might happen!

The village runs up a hillside, and when at length we arrived breathless at the top, we found indeed a fine Venetian tower—square, three-storeyed, with all the V-shaped merlons of its roof battlements intact. It was a good specimen of the towers that are scattered everywhere through this part of the island—but it could not possibly be any part of the castle of La Cuppa.

We looked round anxiously; and at last Aileen imagined that she could make out what might be a fragment of wall on a distant hill. A woman had paused to watch us curiously, and I now asked her if she knew of any castle ruins in the neighbourhood. She broke into a strident patter of Greek; and from a word or two that I managed to catch, combined with her gestures, I gathered there *was* a castro, but that it was quite impossible to reach it. On the other hand, there was a superb monastery not very far away to which a car would take us. We ought to go there. I persisted that, foolishly, we wanted the castro. Her Greek then became a torrent that swept me from all hope of grasping anything. She saw this, and her flying hands began to mime a pioneer struggling through vegetation head-high, and I had a vision of some forgotten stronghold buried in the jungle, and rapidly becoming a legend.

Her voice had attracted more women, and we were now surrounded. All of them talked, shrilly and with determination, partly at us and partly to one another, and Aileen and I exchanged helpless glances. I raised my hand; they stopped and I repeated my wish to go to the castro. Whereupon the racket broke out again; and I didn't need to understand a word to realize that here was a Greek chorus following the canonic tradition and prophesying the direst consequences.

At this crisis, when there seemed nothing for it but to disengage as quickly as we could, Aileen had an inspiration. It is indeed at these moments, when, deafened by the incomprehensible, and maddened by inability to vent the eloquence that is rising within me, I am about to throw in my hand—it is often at such a moment that she reveals a knack of uttering a word that is occult in its effect. In this case, pointing to a tethered mule, and then to the hill where we imagined our castle to be, she merely ejaculated: 'Moulári.'

The babel ended abruptly. If we were talking of hiring mules, it was quite a different matter, it was business—in which there are no impossibilities, only a price for removing them.

An urgent summons brought up a woman who spoke English. She confirmed that there was a castro on the hill. I said that as it appeared the way was difficult, I was prepared to hire a guide. Mules, we decided, would be too expensive. The women went into conference, and presently, one of them reluctantly permitted herself to be thrust forward as a volunteer for the perilous job. The English-speaker, who was now the acknowledged leader of the chorus, demanded 100 drachmae for the guide. I agreed to this; but I was not now dealing with happy-go-lucky males, who are willing to commit all to a 'gentleman's agreement': there is no such thing as a 'lady's agreement', and she demanded to see the colour of my money, or rather the denomination of my notes. I showed her a 100 drachmae note.

A general stir of relief ran through the chorus.

'She will guide you well,' said the leader. 'She is a good girl.' She looked me sternly in the eye, and repeated: 'A very good girl.'

I hastened to express my appreciation of having anyone so good with us; and hoped we could now start.

The good girl, who was barefooted, ran to fetch shoes from her house, and when she returned, she brought a man—whether as a protector, or to make sure I paid up, or because two heads are better than one when there is some doubt of the way, I never knew.

The four of us set out, down a lane handsomely lined with chaste-trees flowering in long, blue spikes, and on through a flat expanse carpeted with the thick autumn tangle of Greek fields—dried thistles, at intervals a dog onion swaggering with its tall white panache, Jerusalem sage, which the Greeks call *spháka*, and which is said to give off a fine dust that irritates the eyes; the unexpected, friendly glow of heather in bloom, and much else. Soon, however, the ground began to climb, grew stony, and was plentifully littered with prickly oak and low thorn bushes. The going, nevertheless, was not at all difficult, and there was nothing to justify the picture evoked by the women. Until, after we had been walking for about an hour and a half, and were near the summit of the hill, we were faced by a steep rise covered by giant boulders, with thick undergrowth between them.

The good girl had never ceased to talk to the man throughout the climb—a remarkable feat that we, panting behind, could fully appreciate. The man, merely grunting perfunctorily at intervals, had plodded on in the lead; now, among the boulders, he was evidently at fault, and her monologue rose into a siren wail proclaiming danger. He showed no alacrity to tackle the boulders; so, goaded by the imminence of the summit, I went ahead doggedly. Aileen followed; and the guides joined in behind. And after quite a scramble, we reached the top.

There was no castle to be seen. Only a small chapel.

That, anyway, was our first impression; but looking about more carefully, we came to a different conclusion. The summit was a narrow, oblong, boulder-strewn ridge, about eighty yards in length, from which the ground dropped sharply on all sides except the east, where a col ran to a hill that dominated our summit. The chapel occupied a rocky platform at the highest, central point of the ridge: it had a tiny apse at the east with an arrow-slit window, and although it had apparently been recently restored, or perhaps rebuilt, its stones were old. Abutting on it to the west were the ends of two walls; at the eastern point of the oblong were the ruins of a square tower, with one wall reaching a height of about twelve feet; and in the centre of the northern boundary of the ridge were the remains of another tower. That was all.

We wandered round, rather disgruntled; but experience had taught us that a Greek castle, confronted by our prying eyes, is always apt to emulate the Baker confronted by a Boojum, and suddenly vanish away—owing to the fact that the Greeks are prone to call any fragment of masonry a castro, leaving one in doubt as to whether this is due to a long memory or a vivid imagination. We concluded there had been a castle here, but whether it were La Cuppa was a different matter. The location is, I believe, approximately right; but the area is very small, and although these castles have invariably been quarried over the centuries by the neighbouring people, I would still have expected to find more of it. The fact that the name, La Cuppa, rang no bell with the locals probably does not mean much, since names are quickly lost or transformed.

The good girl talked all the way down: only when I paid the agreed money did she stop—astonished, I imagined, beyond words at the inexplicable interests of foreigners. Or perhaps what took away her breath was that, having made the bargain with her, I felt it was only right to offer her the money, and not the man. She could only gesture tongue-tied towards the magnificent male. He may have been her husband; if so, I was glad he had the money; he needed any compensation he could get, for by this time I had come to sympathize with Milton's Satan who felt 'how awful goodness is'!

The castle of La Cuppa is connected with the story of

24

Licario, the poor gentleman of Kárystos, who became one of the most brilliant commanders of the thirteenth century, and worked such harm to his compatriots. Licario's immediate forbears had come from Vicenza soon after the Latin conquest of Euboea; they had settled at Kárystos in the south of the island, and there Licario had been brought up. About, or shortly before, the year 1270, he left Kárystos, and went to Negroponte, as a member of the household of Gilbert dalle Carceri da Verona, the brother of the triarch of central Euboea. Gilbert had a sister, Dame Felisa, a young widow, who was living, together with her small son, in her brother's palace; and Licario fell violently in love with her.

He was a good-looking fellow, with dark chestnut hair, a golden tan, and fine eyes; and if he was a little rough in his manners, he had a graceful bearing, and was by no means a boor, since he appears to have been as fond of study as he was of arms.[5] At any rate, Felisa returned his love, and eventually they entered into a clandestine marriage. For some time they were able to keep their secret, but at length the suspicions of Gilbert's wife were aroused, and the truth was discovered. Immediately the wrath of Gilbert, and the whole dalle Carceri clan, fell upon this penniless nobody who had dared to ally himself with one of them. He had to leave Felisa, and fly for his life from Negroponte.

He went back to Kárystos, gathered about him a band of discontented young men, made a rude stronghold for himself in the hills in an exposed position known as Anemopylae, or 'the gates of the wind', and set up as an outlaw. In this, as in everything he undertook, he was very successful; and soon he and his 'black bonnets', as they were called, had all the surrounding peasantry terrorized and abjectly subservient. But that was not nearly enough for him: he was ambitious and confident, and above all, he burned to revenge himself on the dalle Carceri. So, taking the quickest means to this end, he turned traitor, and offered his services to the Greek Emperor. The Emperor, Michael VIII Palaiologos, glad of any stick to beat the Latins, received these overtures graciously; and Licario was invited to Constantinople, where he promised the Emperor that, if he were given the forces, he would reduce the whole island of Euboea. Evidently, Michael was impressed by the young man: he supplied the men—and Licario made good his word.

Carrying on a vigorous guerrilla war in the island, he captured Oreos in the north, and later, the castle of La Cuppa. So well did he do that William de Villehardouin, Prince of Achaia and suzerain of the barons of Euboea, became alarmed; and in 1272 he, and Dreux de Beaumont, marshal of Charles of Anjou, King of Sicily, led an army to the help of the barons. De Beaumont was defeated at Oreos, but William, the experienced veteran, recaptured La Cuppa from Licario, who for the time being was compelled to remain quiet. But three years later his opportunity came.

At that date war had broken out between the Greek independent state of Neopatras in Thessaly, and the Byzantine Empire. The ruler of Neopatras had been driven out before the invading imperial army; but John, Duke of Athens, came to his assistance with a handful of horsemen. There were perhaps 500 of them, and they found themselves confronting an army of some 30,000. It was, however, a very mixed force with a number of mercenaries, and Duke John, looking at it, quoted Herodotus to his companions: 'Many men, but few soldiers'. In the approved tradition, he told his men that any of them who didn't care for the odds could retire; but only two did so. The others, led by the Duke, thundered down on the Greek host, and routed it completely. It was another of those victories against astronomical odds of which the Franks in Greece have several to their credit.

No sooner did the barons of Euboea hear of this triumph than they determined to emulate it on the sea, and destroy the Greek fleet that was stationed to the north of Euboea, off Demetrias, in the Gulf of Volo. But after a hard fight, in which they at first held the advantage, they were defeated with considerable loss, and all but two of their ships were taken by the enemy.

It was Licario's moment.

Euboea was greatly weakened by this disaster, and Licario immediately pressed on with his war. Gilbert's brother had fallen in the sea fight. Gilbert succeeded him as triarch, and was now one of the chief commanders in the field against his renegade brother-in-law. But he was out-fought. Licario began with an ambitious attempt to take the formidable Castel Rosso, or Red Castle, that stood, and still stands, on a hill above his native Kárystos. It was defended by a Burgundian noble, Othon de Cicon, and held out for a considerable time against all attacks by sea and land: but in the end it fell to a blockade.

It was a great prize, and the Greek Emperor now rained favours on Licario. He invested him with the whole of Euboea as his fief, on condition that he maintained 200 knights in the imperial service; and, since poor Felisa had now died, the Emperor bestowed on him for wife a wealthy and aristocratic Greek lady. He was also given command of a fleet, and after he had captured several more castles, including La Cuppa, he put out with his ships, and ravaged the Aegean.

The island of Skopelos was owned by a Ghisi, who was wont to boast in the phrase of Ovid: 'I am too big a man to be harmed by Fortune'; but Licario took both Ghisi and his island, and swept on to pluck a dozen other islands from the Latins. But at Lemnos, he met with a determined resistance, at first from Paolo Navigajoso, and later from Paolo's widow. For three years the island stronghold held out, and then the lady 'departed with all the corn in the granaries, the lead off the palace roof, and the clothing and money in the castle'.[6]

Long before this, however, Licario was back in Euboea, meditating an even greater coup—nothing less than an attack on the capital, Negroponte.

But that story is more closely connected with the castle of Filla, to which we shall come.

Not finding much to interest us in Avlonarion, we returned

to the bus stop on the main road, and found we had an hour and a half to wait. We sat at the café under a mulberry tree, drank coffee, and watched the life of the hamlet—represented at the moment by two elderly, barefooted males in dirty rags, one of whom toiled at transporting across the road, bit by bit, the huge pieces of some ancient and mysterious machine. He reminded me of those ants of Robert Graves'

> '. . . who undertake
> Gigantic loads for honour's sake';

while the other, a true grasshopper, contented himself with looking on. By way of diversion they argued. Presently, the radio in a nearby kiosk broke into dance music, and the grasshopper, shuffling his bare feet in the dust, danced happily, while the ant, plodding on, made caustic remarks; and so they fell again to arguing. Hardly as idyllic as the life on Keats' Grecian urn, but at least nearly as static.

The woman who owned the café came to chat with us, and took us into her garden, where she presented us with a large aubergine, and where Aileen became fascinated by a castor oil tree with enormous palmate leaves marked with red veins, and seeds that are rather like cowrie shells. So fascinated that we nearly missed our bus, which arrived and drove off almost at once. We tore through the house, and down the street, shouting madly. Everyone within earshot shouted with us—and the driver pulled up. Blessed is the land where bus-drivers are still human, and not outcast from the race by the curse of bell and clock and the book of regulations!

All the same, the journey back was a nightmare!

The bus radio was turned on to the limit of its volume control, and either the set was not properly tuned in, or it was not very selective, for we had a hideous medley of two stations, and two wailing sopranos. As an accompaniment, the driver sounded his horn with infuriating frequency, more, I think, out of joie de vivre than for any practical reason; and we rolled through that quiet countryside moaning and bellowing like a beast in pain—the uproar reaching a peak whenever we met another car, which inevitably bore down on us with its horn screaming a challenge to ours.

All this, however, I could have endured with reasonable equanimity, for the Greek love of noise is something we have had to abide on innumerable occasions; but next to me sat a Greek afflicted with the usual avid curiosity—and he spoke no English. Striving through the bedlam to catch from him a word I could understand, and yelling at the top of my voice in reply, I had to endure the catechism: Where did we come from? Was this my wife? How long had we been married? And finally of course the great status-determining question: How many children had we? Hoarse, deafened, raging and helpless, I clutched our aubergine to my bosom, and longed to hurl it at his head, while, with the few vestiges of decency remaining in me, I tried not to glower at him. Aileen, who was of course not expected to join in this get-together, made full use of her immunity, and clamping a fixed smile on her face, sank into a defensive coma.

It was a long, long way to Chalcis.

The next morning the meltémi, the north to north-east wind that prevails in the Aegean during the summer months, was blowing. A cold, uncomfortable wind, when it blows so late in the year, it prodded up the Euripus, which bared its teeth, and flung itself irritably against the quay, and it blew all the gaiety out of the promenade: the coloured chairs and tables were piled up to prevent their being overturned; the awnings were furled; the charcoal braziers were under hatches; while the little old victoria with its drooping horse had turned its back to the blast, and seemed to cower in dread of being blown away. Only the row of drying octopuses, flirting their tentacles wildly, like the corps de ballet in a Disney fantasy, added a touch of grotesque hilarity. The promenade, stripped bare, piled with 'props', and occupied by the single, decrepit, period vehicle, might have been the stage of Victorian barnstormers, after they had gone broke, and packed their scenery for a getaway, while the manager, hunched and dejected under the hood of his cab, took a last look at his ruin!

We hurried off and caught a bus to the little village of Belizia, which is the stop nearest to the castle of Alivérion. A pleasant walk of half an hour through olive groves, and over the brow of a small hill, brought us in sight of the castle.

I have not been able to discover anything of its history, but it is worth a visit if only for the charm of its appearance; for, looked at from the rise on which we stood, it represented exactly what one's fancy had pictured as the typical castle in the Aegean. A scrub-dotted hill rose in a neat cone with the castle perched on its apex, background and foreground were dashed in with three broad strips of colour, light blue sky, dark blue sea, saffron land, and created a design as simplified and boldly effective as the cover of a travel brochure.

The ascent to it was easy; and we walked up through a guard of honour provided by tall dog onions, drawn up at intervals on either side of the track. There was a fair amount of the castle left. Roughly rectangular, with its short side parallel to the sea, which lay on the south, the enclosure was divided into two by the ruins of a square keep with an adjoining wall. Within, the most notable feature was a pointed arch in the dividing wall, which allowed the chemin-de-ronde, or wall-walk, to pass through; this alone, amid all the disordered rubble, the jagged masonry and gaping breaches, still preserved a touch of elegance, and recalled an aristocratic past.

Above the lower courses, rudely squared oblong blocks mingled with tile and rubble predominated, and from this one might deduce that the castle was probably a Turkish reconstruction; but it is a difficult business to date the portions of a Greek castle. Most of them have been continuously repaired by Greeks, Latins and Turks throughout their existence, and the occupants were often inclined to imitate the work of their predecessors, so that few dates can be given with any certainty. I regret this, for it seems to me that in history, which Napoleon defined as an agreed fable, dates have a reassuring firmness about them, and for my part, I like to have plenty around. I am grateful to those who salvage dates for us, and even to those who make a gallant attempt at it, such as Dr John Lightfoot who, in 1642, affirmed that the world 'was created by the Trinity on October 23rd 4004 B.C. at nine o'clock in the morning'. The Doctor may have been wrong, but he had, I feel, the right approach to history!

There was a good view along the coast westward, somewhat marred by the town of Alivérion, which sprawled down to the sea a mile or two away; but beyond it were the hills. In Euboea distance seems to lend its most effective enchantment, and to clothe the hills in pastel shades that have the very aura of gentleness and benevolence; but it is all a deception—as one may see here on the south-east, where the hills draw close, and reveal themselves as barren and harsh. Yet a single deserted road, passing below the castle, wound into them, and seemed to promise a village somewhere among those arid heights. On the whole it was an excellent situation for an Euboean baron, with good facilities for piracy, effective control over the surrounding country, and, if it came to the worst, an escape route into the hills.

About four o'clock we returned to Belizia, and sat down at a café a short distance beyond the bus stop. The proprietor told us the next bus to Chalcis was at six; so resignedly we ordered drinks, and composed ourselves to wait. No sooner had the drinks arrived than we heard a bus approaching. The proprietor smiled. This, he explained soothingly, was the Athens bus. As we knew, the Athens bus does not go to Chalcis, but to Nea Psara, where it connects with a ferry to the mainland; so we relaxed again, and fondled our drinks. But buses in Greece are, in one respect, as the wind, and one ought never to be sure that a Greek, even though he hears the sound thereof, can tell whence it comes or whither it goes. In this case it swung into view round the corner, bearing in front the one word 'XAΛKIS'. We sprang up, grabbed our belongings, abandoned our drinks, and once more ran shouting down the street. . . .

Again we were lucky. It was the same bus that had picked us up the day before; and after he had gone round collecting fares, the conductor, dropping his official manner, returned to shake us warmly by the hand, as though we were old friends. A ceremony repeated by the driver at the terminus.

One is always encountering these little gestures in Greece, for the Greeks have the most engaging manners of any people I have met; always easy and natural, they have the knack of being polite with a flourish, and yet of conveying a sincerity that is the essence of courtesy. If they cross-examine the stranger in a tiresome way, this is by no means only curiosity, but owes a good deal to a conviction that the host ought to take a kindly interest in the guest; for it is not their least endearing trait that they tend to look on every visitor as a guest, and the tourist with experience of other countries is constantly astonished to find in the Greek provinces that his delight in the scene is regarded not merely as a fortunate eccentricity to be exploited, but as a sincere compliment that merits a friendly return. I do not say the tourist is never exploited, but it is a rare event, and he continually meets with extraordinary kindness.

The next day we had another example of this.

There had been a shower of rain in the evening after the meltémi had dropped, but the morning was brilliant again, and we made for the castle of Filla, which lies six or more miles east of Chalcis. Our bus took us first to Basilikon, on the main road to Alivérion, and then, turning north, ran for a mile or two through a thickly-wooded stretch of country, which was quite a surprise in these parts.

Filla is only a small village, and, seeking directions for the best way up to the castle, we went to the main kapheneíon, where the proprietor came out to talk to us. He was a magnificent looking veteran—tall, with a soldierly uprightness, a handsome old face, a fine white moustache, and a gravely courteous manner. Put him in the traditional dress, with Albanian bonnet, fustanella, pomponned shoes and a long musket, and he would have been the typical klepht warrior.

He was as gracious as he was handsome. He insisted on coming with us, and leading us through the village to the path that ascended the bare hill on which the castle stood. With the castle in full view, I endeavoured to persuade him that he could now safely let us proceed on our own. It was no use, he remained watching us anxiously, as we went up; and when we diverged a little from the track, he was after us in a twinkling, and we could only follow him meekly for the rest of the way.

He remained while we inspected everything, made notes and plans, and took photographs; then he led us down to his café. He brought us to the courtyard at the back, where a windlass stood over a well, steps ran up to the second storey, flowers grew round the perimeter in beds and in tall white tubs, and a great vine, from which hung innumerable bunches of grapes, spread over a pergola and gave shade. He put us down at a table, and his wife came to attend upon us—a quiet little woman, whose plain face attracted by its kindliness. They gave us bread and cheese, and grapes that they cut from the vine, and we drank portokalátha, a Greek form of orangeade that to my mind beats all the drinks of the country, except possibly the water. Presently, when her husband had entered the house for a moment, the wife shyly offered a bunch of flowers to Aileen, and sat down at the table to chat; but directly he returned, she rose. Yet one was aware that this was not through awe of him, but simply the traditional manners, now happily disappearing, that require this deference in the women of a household.

We learnt laboriously a little of his history. He had been seven years in the army, had seen service in the world war, and had been twice wounded by the communists in the civil war that followed. He showed us photographs of his two brothers in America, and asked rather wistfully about boat and air fares; it was apparent that age had in no way subdued his spirit, that if in his campaigning he had seen a little of the world, he was still eager to see more, even, possibly, to transplant himself to another land. Restless in this tiny village, he looked upon us, I felt, less as tourists, than as an embassy from the fabulous West of his dreams.

We sat talking until our bus arrived; and then as we left, they gave us each a sprig of basil from a plant in the house.

In that delightful book, In *Argolis*, George Horton writes: 'To present anyone with a bunch of basil means, "I am glad to see you". It is hard to find a Greek house without one or more basil pots in it, and it is the invariable custom to break off a sprig and hand it to each welcome guest.'[7] Another traveller, Theodore Bent, has written of the powers attributed to basil in Greece:

> 'The herb, which they say grew on Christ's grave, is almost worshipped in the Eastern Church. On St Basil's Day women take sprigs of this plant to be blessed in church. On returning home they cast some on the floor of the house to ensure luck for the ensuing year. They eat a little with their household, and no sickness, they maintain, will attack them for a year. Another bit they put into their cupboard, and firmly believe that their embroideries and silken raiment will be free from the visitation of rats, mice and moths for the same period.'[8]

Bent was writing in the 1880s, and Horton over sixty years ago, but you will still see basil in many houses, and we were delighted to find the custom of giving a sprig to the visitor was still kept up.

At parting, the old man took my hand in both of his, and pressed it earnestly to convey his good wishes in the only way in which he could be sure I would understand; and after that he stood waving until we were out of sight.

The castle of Filla is another associated with Licario. In 1276, supported by a Greek fleet, and a number of Catalan mercenaries, he made a feint of attacking Negroponte, and, as he anticipated, the Latin garrison, contemptuous of the renegade and his mixed force, sallied out against him. They were headed by Duke John of Athens, who had led his horsemen to victory against such enormous odds at Neopatras. He was gouty, and not very firm in the saddle, but he advanced as dauntlessly as ever; and at his side rode the triarch, Gilbert da Verona, brother of Felisa, and the bitter enemy of Licario. They drove Licario before them to a point about six miles north of Negroponte, where the village of Vatondas now stands; and there he led them into an ambush. They fought fiercely, but they had been completely out-manoeuvred, and the battle went in favour of the Greeks. Duke John was wounded and unhorsed, and he and Gilbert were both taken.

It seemed that Negroponte must now fall; but it was saved by the energy of the Venetian Bailie, Morosini Rosso, and by a superb forced march made by Duke John's cousin, Jacques de la Roche. Jacques governed Argos and Nauplia in the Peloponnesus for the Duke, and as soon as he heard of Licario's triumph, he assembled his men, and marched from Nauplia to Chalcis, a distance of about 126 miles, in the astonishing time of twenty-four hours. That secured the city; while the defeat of a Greek army on the mainland by the ruler of Neopatras further relieved the pressure.

Licario retired to Filla, but he was a happy man—his revenge was all he could have dreamed. Shortly, he set out for Constantinople to meet the Emperor, taking his two distinguished prisoners in chains. As for the haughty Gilbert, his feelings are revealed in what followed; for if we are to believe the Byzantine chronicler Nicephorus Gregoras, Gilbert, held at the door of the imperial audience chamber, found it more than he could bear to watch this upstart, his former servant, dressed in the robes of a high office, chatting familiarly with the Emperor. In the words of a modern French historian, 'struck to the heart by the insolence of fate', he fell dead on the threshold of the room.[9]

One wonders if Licario were a little annoyed, if he felt

perhaps his enemy had had the last word; for there was something not unromantic, not unworthy of high tragedy, in thus
dying so palpably of a broken heart—it was an exit that would
be remembered.

Licario went back to Filla. He was now master of the whole
island outside the walls of Negroponte, and his rule was, as
usual, a reign of terror; but he did not remain there long.
Soon he became Lord High Admiral of the Byzantine Empire,
with the title of 'Grand Duke'; and embarking on another
cruise, he plundered the islands of Seriphos and Siphnos, and
did not hesitate to make inroads on the coast of the Duchy
of Athens itself, now under the rule of Duke William. Then,
quite suddenly, Licario ceases to be. What happened, or when
he died, or how, we do not know. He simply disappears. To
be succeeded in the post of Lord High Admiral by a pirate chief,
John de lo Cavo of the island of Anaphê.

Licario had dealt his countrymen a tremendous blow; he
had taken from them almost the whole of Euboea, and a great
many of the Aegean islands; and his triumphs might have
altered all the subsequent history of these places. As it happened, however, there was to be a sequel, provided by a
character whose career was no less spectacular than Licario's.
His name was Bonifacio da Verona, and we shall meet him
at Kárystos.

Our approach to Filla brought us before the north-west
curtain, in which is the main gate. Painted in enormous white
letters on the wall was the word O X I, meaning 'No', a
reminder of 28th October 1940, the day on which the Greeks
said 'No' to the Italian ultimatum—a day now celebrated
annually in Greece.

A pity, we felt, to have disfigured the old castle with this
giant graffito; but the Greeks have a peculiar liking for slogans
writ large. On a previous trip we had passed an army barracks
outside Sparta that was girdled by patriotic sentiments in
huge letters made of whitewashed stones; and later, at the
castle of Amphissa, we found the gateway decorated with a

whitewashed quotation from Thucydides on one side, and one from Homer on the other.

Filla is in the shape of an irregular pentagon, whose walls, from the outside, appear reasonably intact, except on the north-east. To the right as one approaches from the north-west, is the first gate, leading into a narrow alley between the main curtain and an outer wall: at the end of this, another gate, which has now gone, once gave access to the enclosure at its western corner—occupied by the keep. This is the main relic, the walls upstanding with their merlons; next to it is a lower hall with a breach marking a doorway to the enclosure, and elsewhere on the circumference is the wreck of two chambers, one of which had a cistern beneath the floor.

It is a castle that is hardly in keeping with the brilliant and dominating Licario: a small, inconsiderable huddle of masonry on a height that is too easily climbed on all sides, it has no great strength, nor much of a martial air. Some of these veteran holds girn at you with their broken teeth, still fierce, if decrepit, watchdogs, but Filla is humble and staid, and even the merlons might very well be a row of chimneys on the bombed ruin of a village hall. No doubt Licario chose it for its proximity to Negroponte.

But it offered fine views. To the north, across the waves of purple-brown ridges, Dhirfis humped itself against the sky like a leaping dolphin; while to the north-west, beyond Filla village, there was that unusual expanse of wood, an alien rather sinister incursion flooding the whole plain, breaking through a gap in the hills to the sea, and held at bay only by a tall mound in its midst, on which stood twin Venetian towers. Conspicuous in the landscape, they rose above the dark forest in neat symmetry, and the scene might have been the backcloth for some folk-tale melodrama of the Euboean Brothers.

Aileen found a rock-rose trailing from the wall of the cistern; and in the enclosure were many mulleins, which the Greeks call contemptuously *phlomos*, including in this term other plants they think useless. Outside, we came across cyclamens, which in Crete and Italy are known as 'sow bread', because pigs like to root them up; and there, too, was heliotrope, with its small white flowers and grey-green leaves, of which Tournefort aptly notes that 'all the Branches end in an Ear like a Scorpion's Tail'.

Back once more at Chalcis, we were welcomed at the bus station as old and valued clients, and invited round behind the counter for an intimate discussion of our requirements— or maybe it was only that we were holding up the other customers who were buying tickets! We booked on the Kárystos bus leaving at six o'clock the next morning.

It was a perfect evening, and we strolled northward along the Euripus—looking in vain for any sign of dolphins, such as had entertained Dr Sibthorp on a similar calm evening in October 1794. The Doctor, intent on botanizing, or 'simpling' as they liked to call it, sailed down the Euripus in a caique, with the dolphins playing round his ship, while the *carabokyri*, or skipper, whistled to them in the manner of Arion—but not, Dr Sibthorp tells us emphatically, with Arion's skill. The *carabokyri* was, I fancy, an equally incompetent captain: at any rate, the Doctor, after taking a walk ashore at Chalcis, returned to the ship to find 'the bottom of the mainmast, which was made of silver fir, so completely decayed that our carabokyri was obliged to call in the assistance of a ship-carpenter'.[10] An appealing incident; for how beautifully easy-going must be the skipper who fails to observe that his mast is rotting away, and only when it is all but gone is startled into a 'My goodness, my mainmast!' reaction!

Chapter Three

EUBOEA

Bonifacio the Favourite

WE were up at four thirty, and caught our bus at six, having managed to get a few rolls for breakfast at a baker's shop near the bus station. The distance from Chalcis to Kárystos is about seventy miles, and there is plenty of variety in it. Amárinthos in the early morning was looking exquisite—not a ripple on the sea, not a flutter in the awnings, not a human being in sight: it was asleep, or perhaps it was entranced, and either way it seemed unmannerly to go buzzing through it like a bluebottle round the Sleeping Beauty.

At Alivérion we had to change buses, and were spotted by our friend, the conductor of yesterday's bus: we shook hands again with warmth and ceremony——it had now, I felt, become a symbolic, hands-across-the-sea rite, demonstrating Anglo-Greek unity to the world! Yet it was not embarrassing, for one soon grows accustomed, when words fail one, to living a hand for mouth existence.

The road turns inland after Alivérion, and, at Lepoura, branches south-east, climbs a ridge, and drops into a wide grassy plain, a great bowl in the hills on which sheep graze. Really this is the bed of Lake Dhistos, which in winter, I believe, is a sheet of water; but now there were only a few pools, and, lush and green and oddly unlike a Greek landscape, it might have been a part of that sixth continent, Romney Marsh.

Presently, as we climbed again, the tall feathery rushes and

39

wild red daphne by the roadside fell away, and we entered barren and broken hills, dotted with prinári, or the prickly kermes oak, and the evergreen bushes, or mastic trees, the Greeks call schínos. But the spade and plough had edged in where they could: there were stretches of terracing on which were growing vegetables, while a round threshing floor, or alóni, showed that corn was also produced.

Beyond the narrowest part of the island, where it is possible to catch a glimpse of the sea on each side, we approached Stíra, and I looked anxiously but in vain for any sign of the castle of Larmena, which is somewhere in the neighbourhood.

Larmena comes into the Licario story, and saw a certain amount of fighting in the thirteenth century; but a more recent battle took place at Stíra, when, in 1822 during the War of Independence, Elias Mavromichalis, leading a force of Greeks to the blockade of Kárystos, encountered the Turks here. Elias was the eldest son of Petrobey, the old feudal chief of the Maina; and Elias's younger brother, George, and his uncle, Constantine, became notorious nine years later when they murdered the Greek president, Capodistrias, at Nauplia.

Elias was defeated by the Turks; but he and a few men refused to retreat, and shutting themselves up in an old windmill near Stíra, they defended it valiantly while their ammunition lasted. Elias then attempted to cut his way out, sword in hand, but was shot and killed.

Next to arrive on the scene, also bound, at the head of 700 men, for the siege of Kárystos, was the celebrated guerrilla chief, Odysseus—of whom his still more famous brother-in-law, 'Younger Son' Trelawny, has written: 'Descended from the most renowned race of Klephtes, he was a master of the art of mountain warfare, and a thorough Greek in cunning; strong-bodied, nimble-footed, and nimble-witted'.[1] He was also, if one may judge from his subsequent behaviour at Kárystos, a little nimble in his loyalty.

It is an odd thing that Euboea is always reminding the Briton of home; I have mentioned the Dhistos depression, and now, on a plateau above Stíra, we came upon a Scottish moor, with miles of heather, a few drystone boundaries, and even a 'muir-burn' in operation.

Kárystos, with its pleasant, tree-shaded *platea* fronting the sea, strikes one as more spacious and better planned than the usual run of Greek ports, which, if they lie white and beautiful as foam at the edge of the blue water, owe hardly anything of their loveliness to deliberate design. Kárystos attempts style.

It was the season when it was waiting for the wine from the vintage, and all along the front, ranks of barrels were drawn up with here and there a monster barrel towering above the rest. These monsters had a grotesque air that gave the prospect of barrels a hint of carnival; and I wondered whether this happy event were celebrated with fiddles and dancing on the quay and wine running down the gutters! So far as I can hear, there is no Dionysian revelry; but it was certainly a sight to stimulate Captain Stratton's fancy!

We walked into an hotel along the front, to find it entirely deserted. It was a little after eleven o'clock in the morning, so there was no question of the siesta; the door was open, everything looked spick and span, but we had it all to ourselves. 'Is there anybody there?' we cried, like De la Mare's Traveller, and stood 'perplexed and still' when there was no answer. At the back was a terraced garden as empty as the house; but while we debated the etiquette of the problem, there was a stir in the shrubbery, and a young woman materialized.

She said nothing, but beckoned us up an outside stair, waved us into a bedroom, and departed. We never saw anyone again, until we left. No one else was staying in the hotel; no staff was ever apparent; our room was tidied, the beds made, and the hotel was always neat and clean, but for all we saw, it might have been the work of the Brownies after midnight. And when the time came to leave this enchanted inn, I thought it conceivable we might have to lay the money for our bill on the mantelpiece.

Emerging into the blazing sunshine, we made our way to

the hill behind the town, on which stands Castel Rosso. (Plate II)

Kárystos has a new look today, but it is in fact an ancient town. In the third book of the *Odyssey*, Nestor relates how on returning from Troy he put in at night with his ships to Kárystos, and 'There on the altar of Poseidon we laid many thighs of bulls, thankful to have traversed the great sea'.[2] Homer also mentions that Elphenor led the men of Kárystos to Troy; and Strabo says the town was noted for asbestos and marble; but it acquired more importance in the early days of the Frankish conquest. Then, in the first decade of the thirteenth century, the three triarchates of Euboea fell to Ravano dalle Carceri who became sole ruler of the island, and built Castel Rosso at Kárystos, on the hill that is the site of the ancient Greek acropolis. The castle came to the Burgundian noble, Othon de Cicon, and we have seen how it was taken from him by the Greeks under Licario about the year 1276. It remained in Greek hands for twenty years, and then it was recaptured for the Latins by another dalle Carceri.

The events leading up to this have been well described by the old Catalan chronicler, Ramon Muntaner, who was personally acquainted with the people concerned. He tells how a certain Bonifacio dalle Carceri da Verona, who was the youngest son of his parents and owned but a single castle in Italy, sold the castle, equipped himself in gentlemanly style with the proceeds, and came to the Duchy of Athens, where he had an elder brother to whom he looked for advancement. But he found his brother had just died, and although Bonifacio became very friendly with the Duke of Athens, and made a considerable show at Thebes, where the Duke held his court, he fell heavily into debt.

At this time the Duke, Guy II, the last de la Roche ruler, was a minor; but on St John the Baptist's day 1294 he came of age, and a brilliant ceremony was held at Thebes to mark the occasion, and to confer on the Duke the order of knighthood. Muntaner describes it:

'The day of the court came and in all the court no one was better dressed and more splendidly than micer Bonifazio and his retinue, and he had full a hundred torches with his device; and the money for all this he borrowed on the allowance he was to receive later. What shall I tell you? A great feast began. And when they were in the cathedral where the Duke was to be knighted, the archbishop said mass and the arms of the Duke were on the altar, and all men were in expectation of the Duke being dubbed knight, and wondered, thinking the King of France and the Emperor had a dispute, for each would think it a great honour that the Duke should wish to be knighted by his hand. And as all were thus waiting, he had micer Bonifazio of Verona called, and he came at once and the Duke said to him:—"Micer Bonifazio, sit here, by the side of the archbishop, for I wish that you dub me knight". And micer Bonifazio said:—"Ah, my Lord, what are you saying? Are you mocking me?" "Assuredly not," said the Duke, "I wish it to be thus." And micer Bonifazio, who saw that he meant to stand by what he said, approached the archbishop at the altar and there he dubbed the Duke knight. And when he had dubbed him knight, the Duke said before all:—"Micer Bonifazio, it is the custom that those who dub a knight always give a present to the new knight they have made. But I wish to do quite the opposite; you have made me knight, wherefore I give you here fifty thousand sueldos torneses of yearly income forever, from this day onward, to you and yours, all in castles and important places and free fiefs, to do as you like. And again I give you to wife the daughter of a certain baron who has remained in my power, and who is mistress of the third part of the island and city of Negroponte." And so see how he endowed him in one day and in one hour, for it was the most splendid gift any prince had made in one day for a long time and it was a new and strange thing. And thereafter micer Bonifazio lived rich and wealthy, and the Duke, in dying, left the care of his soul to him and made him procurator of the Duchy until the arrival of the count of Brienne.'[3]

The lady whom the Duke bestowed on Bonifacio was Agnes de Cicon, the heiress of Kárystos and Aegina; but her castle at Kárystos, Castel Rosso, was still in the hands of the Greeks, and Bonifacio now undertook the task of winning it back. Not only was he successful in this, but he also recaptured Larmena; and by the end of the century almost all Licario's conquests had returned to the Latins. Thus did the favourite make good—an event that does not often occur in history—and Bonifacio da Verona become the most important of all the Euboean lords.

The hill on which the castle stands is not steep on the seaward side, but it is rough going, and on the hottest day we had had, we found the ascent a toil. Wilting under that ferocious sun, we were thankful to encounter the shade of a narrow belt of fir trees, whence we emerged eventually at the south-west corner of the castle. This is the best aspect, for the south wall is a noble work: it stands forty to fifty feet high, and it stretches east for about a hundred and fifty feet, from a square bastion at the south-west to the main gate. To look at it is to feel with Bacon that 'it is a reverend thing to see an ancient castle or building not in decay'.

Alas, as one walks along the curtain, one discovers that it is not quite as whole as one thought at the first glance, for the main gate is in ruins; but beyond it the wall continues again for another seventy feet to a fine, seven-sided tower, which has all its V-shaped merlons intact.

To be accurate, this is really the curtain of the second enceinte, because there appears to have been a vast outer enclosure, the wall of which ran in a great arc to the south, passing along the outer edge of the belt of firs. There is not much left of it now, nor of the defence works it enclosed, among which was a square tower with vaulted cisterns beneath it.

We climbed through the ragged breach that was the main

gate, and were at once faced with another disillusionment. Castel Rosso, for all its efforts on this side to keep up appearances, is not only ancient but senile. Everywhere else it has been picked to the bone by Time, and lies a fractured skeleton, with ribs and spines of masonry poking up fantastically to mark where a tower once stood in the mouldering wall. Yet it is dying hard, and one cannot but admire its last desperate attempt, with its back to the wall of hills, to present to the world a frowning martial face—even if the jaws have rather fallen in. In its decline it has lost, too, the ruddiness from which it takes its name, at least we could see no sign of it.

The second enceinte is a rough quadrilateral, cut off at the north-east by a dividing curtain to form a third, or inner enclosure, at a higher level, on which stood the keep in former days. But the only structure remaining there today is a small, whitewashed modern chapel. It is a habit of the Greeks to plant these chapels among castle ruins, and this does not add to the attractions of a site, except when the chapel is a genuine relic that has been restored. Nevertheless, despite their white glare among the grey walls, they are not too disturbing; and it is an engaging notion that these arrogant fortresses, after their centuries of warfare, should in old age emulate Peele's veteran, and exchange their battle cries for holy psalms!

We went up to the highest point of the castle (Plate I), the site of the keep, and looking down the face of the cliff, which on this side drops very steeply, we could see in the valley below some remaining arches of the aqueduct that had formerly brought water into the town, and had probably been broken in 1822 by the besieging Greeks.

The castle was renowned for its strength, and it was reckoned that in its heyday a garrison of no more than thirty men-at-arms could hold it; and indeed history does seem to show that it was never an easy place to storm. After Bonifacio's successful attack on it, its story is concerned for a little both with him, and with the Catalan Grand Company—that band of veteran free-lances who had been thrown out of work in 1302 by the conclusion of the war in Italy between the houses of Aragon and Anjou. The Company was probably the most efficient fighting unit to be found anywhere at the time; indeed, in this respect the Catalans were worthy forerunners of the men who fought under Cortez—who have been reckoned, together with Caesar's Tenth Legion, Napoleon's Old Guard, and Wellington's Light Division, as the greatest soldiers the world has seen.

By 1311 the Company had fought its way from the lands of the Byzantine Empire to the borders of Athens, and here, at the battle of the Kephissos, they almost annihilated the Frankish chivalry of Greece. The slaughter was appalling. Muntaner says that 'of all the seven hundred knights, only two escaped'; and he adds: 'And of those two, one was micer Bonifazio da Verona, lord of the third part of Negroponte who was a very honourable, good man, and had always loved the Company. They saved him as soon as they recognised him'.⁴ As a matter of fact Muntaner was wrong, there were more than two survivors; nevertheless, Frankish Greece was permanently crippled by its losses here.

The 'Fortunate Company of the Catalans' went on to take possession of the Duchy of Athens, and they held it for seventy-six years. In the early days, they were a constant menace to Euboea, which suffered many raids from them, and the Venetians were driven to organize a fleet for its defence, to which the Euboean barons were asked to contribute. All agreed to to do so, except Bonifacio. He had remained on excellent terms with the Catalans; indeed, after Kephissos, they had offered him the leadership of the Company, and he was determined to conciliate rather than to oppose them—after all, he owned thirteen castles in the Duchy, in the territory, that is, of the Company. It is hardly surprising, therefore, that, in 1317, he strengthened his alliance with them by marrying his daughter, Marulla, to the Vicar-General, or ruler of Catalan Athens, Don Fadrique d'Aragon.

Muntaner has left a glowing picture of Marulla. 'I saw her,' he tells us, 'in the house of her father when she was about eight years old'; and he declares she 'was the best lady and the wisest there ever was in that country. And, assuredly, she is one of the most beautiful Christians of the world'.[5] She was the heiress to Castel Rosso and Larmena, as well as to the castles in the Duchy; and when, shortly after the marriage, Bonifacio died, just as the Company had commenced an invasion of Euboea, Fadrique immediately seized Castel Rosso and Larmena in the name of his wife.

Although the Catalans, having taken Negroponte, were forced to withdraw by political pressure, Fadrique continued to hold his two castles. They passed to his son, who lost Castel Rosso to the Genoese, got it back, and finally, in 1365, sold it and Larmena to Venice for 6,000 ducats. It was held for Venice by the Zorzi family, who also came into possession of Boudonitza, the stronghold that guarded the pass of Thermopylae; and when Boudonitza was taken by the Turks in 1414, the last Marquis retired to Castel Rosso, which descended to his son and his grandson, until, in 1470, Negroponte and with it all Euboea fell to the Turks.

Castel Rosso was still strong when the Greeks sat down to besiege it in 1822 in the War of Independence. Having cut off the water supply, they instituted a blockade, and it seemed likely that the Turkish commander, Omer Bey, would be driven to surrender. Suddenly, however, the guerrilla chief, Odysseus, with his 700 men packed up and marched away, and the siege had to be abandoned. Odysseus alleged that his move was due to his running short of provisions; but it was generally believed that he had played a treasonable part, and accepted a bribe from Omer Bey.

The next year he again encountered the Turks near Kárystos, and this time he fought them, having as his ally Mandô Mavroyéni, the heroine of Mykonos, who commanded a company of *palikaris*, which she had raised with the money obtained by selling her jewels. The Greeks won the day; and after the battle, according to the historian Finlay, Odysseus sent fifty heads and three live Turks to Athens—whereupon the Athenians promptly stoned the three to death.[6]

Eventually, of course, the Turks had to give up Castel Rosso; and so, over five hundred years after Bonifacio had driven them out, the Greeks came back.

On our return, we took a slightly different route, and half-way down the hill came upon a large neglected garden. Much overgrown, it was enchantingly green for Greece, its luxuriance being due to water that was led down to it in narrow, open cement channels from some spring higher up. Out in the blazing sun, looking through an iron grille into these cool green vistas, with the faint plash and tinkle of water coming to us, we felt like Dives getting his glimpse of Paradise!

Later, we found the garden belonged to the *patron* of the restaurant we frequented. This restaurant also had a garden in front of it, planted with trees and shrubs, which ought to have been an inviting spot: but for some odd reason, perhaps because we came to it at evening, it was merely dismal. Nor was the restaurant any more cheerful, being a dark cavern of a place that, like the hotel, was always empty. On our first visit, the *patron*, who appeared after an interval, gave us a startled look. Speaking French, he agreed without enthusiasm to provide us with a meal, and we were shown into a more remote, and darker cavern. He went off, and when his footsteps had died away, we waited in silence and gloom with rapidly lowering spirits.

Dragging footsteps sounded at length, and a waiter shuffled in—a sinister-looking type, who eyed us with aversion.

'*Kalispéra!* (Good evening!)' said Aileen, with daring brightness.

He grunted, dropped some cutlery on the table, and shuffled off. We sat there interminably, while the shadows gathered in the garden, and seemed to dim the solitary naked electric bulb overhead. I began to have fancies that the garden was uncanny, that we had stepped through it into the inn at the world's end, that nothing would ever come, that Time was no longer passing on, but passing out . . .

At last the footsteps, as dragging as though they were trailing fetters, started again. They reached our door, and we waited tensely. It turned out to be the food—which was excellent. Moreover, a trifling tip discovered hidden benevolence in the waiter as a divining-rod discovers water, and when we left, even the patron had acquired a custom-built geniality—or perhaps it was just the effect on us of the food. But I always felt that the garden, even at midday, had a foreboding look about it.

In the afternoon we had booked tickets for the boat next day to Andros. This was our first introduction to the business of travelling by steamer among the islands; and it gave us no hint of the exasperating obstacles we should encounter later, for the service from Ruffina, on the Attic coast, to Kárystos and Andros runs daily, and there are few complications. Though even here no-one seemed to know whether or not the boat called at Batsi on Andros. We were anxious to see Batsi, but eventually decided to take tickets to Gavrion, from where there is a bus across the island to Andros town.

The chief difficulty one encounters in navigating the Aegean arises from the fact that an island is on a fixed steamer orbit, that there are several orbits, each including a different series of islands, and that to go from orbit to orbit, without returning to the Piraeus, is always difficult, and sometimes impossible. Travel nowhere in particular and you travel very well; dropping any idée fixe with regard to a destination, and cultivating a cheerful indifference to time, you will be taken without much bother from island to island on an orbit, and will undoubtedly find them all enchanting. But once you give way to the petulant attitude of the young person who complained that she wanted to go to Birmingham and they'd put her down at Crewe, you are heading for trouble and disillusion; while to set out, as Aileen and I did, with a rigid programme of islands on different orbits to be visited, and only a limited time in which to do it, is to gamble recklessly. Of course inter-orbital travel can be done; but directly you inquire as to ways and means, you are up against the same problem as in the matter of buses—everyone has his own idea as to where to catch the boat that catches the boat that reaches the orbit that goes to the island you've set your heart on.

There are other difficulties too. Both the weather and the season induce vagaries in the boats; for in October, when we were travelling, sailings were beginning to be cancelled, and one could never be quite sure if a boat would come as expected. Nor what boat it would be. A not irrelevant point, because in these ports each boat often has its own agent from whom you must get your ticket; and although anyone will direct you to the quayside café where he may be found shortly before the boat arrives, it is advisable, if you are travelling soft, and need a cabin, to book early.

Again, to travel comfortably in these waters, yet as cheaply as possible, requires experience; one has to remember the length of the journey, and the period of the day or night it covers—for there is a time for travelling deck, and for travelling first. In the end, after we had come to know more of the boats, we might also take into account the particular boat in making our decision.

But at Kárystos, Aileen and I were greenhorns in this art of Aegean travel, and our technique was poor. In addition to being of necessity wedded to a destination, we travelled with two suitcases, one of which was heavy, not realizing that in the Aegean lightness is all. One ought to be mobile. Moreover, at many of the islands the ship is unable to make the quay, and if one has to climb down a swaying ladder, and leap in the dark into a rowing boat bobbing on a swell, it is far, far better not to be attached to a heavy suitcase. We decided after this trip that rucksacks were the answer; and they certainly proved to be more manageable, although they tend to upset one's balance slightly at critical moments. I am bound to say, however, that the practice of the islanders themselves is totally different. Every little family group among them travels like an immigrant train, with enough heavy cases and bundles for a string of mules; and somehow, by an inborn or acquired knack, the secret of which I could never fathom, they waft themselves and their belongings on and off the boat in a twinkling. Not without noise; because it is impossible for the Greeks to carry through any operation combining the movements of a number of people, unless everyone shouts at the top of his voice—but without genuine difficulty. While I and that heavy suitcase ricochetted about the ladder in an all-in wrestle.

It was at Kárystos that Aileen was able to satisfy her curiosity about the various builds of caique. They were explained to her by the Greek who kept the little kiosk on the quayside: he had been a sailor, and spoke some English. I fear I cannot interpret his drawings in the correct technical terms; but here is what they meant to my landlubber's eye. A hull with a straight but forward-slanting bow is that of a *perama*; a convex-curved bow indicates a *trehanderi*; and a concave-curved bow, with an undercut stern, a *karavossari*.

Before we left, we explored a small medieval fort, which stands on the shore to the east of the harbour, close to the beginning of the long breakwater. An irregular hexagon, it contains two galleries with embrasures, set one above the other. The roof parapet has its merlons, and on the western wall are two huchettes, or built-out chutes, for pouring down missiles on an enemy attacking the foot of the wall. The effect is of a toylike, preposterous affair, an absurd mingling of merlons, huchettes, and gun embrasures, and one is inclined to label it immediately another Turkish fantasy; but the mixture probably indicates a very early stage of artillery warfare, and it may therefore be of Venetian origin.

Our boat came in shortly after four o'clock and here it was able to make fast to the quay. The journey to Gavrion takes only two hours, and we could have had no better introduction to the Aegean than to steam in this brilliant sunshine along the rugged and desolate coast of Euboea, towards that famous haunt of pirates, the Doro channel.

Chapter Four

ANDROS

The Unfortunate Maria

THE coast of Southern Euboea had a bad reputation in the past. Mr John Hawkins, who voyaged here in 1797, speaking of the Doro channel between Euboea and Andros, remarks:

'This, in fact, is regarded by the Levant sailors as the most dangerous part of their navigation: for there is no sheltered retreat at hand; and the horrors of shipwreck are heightened by the inhospitable character of the natives of this mountainous promontory. Numerous stories are related of their rapacity upon these occasions; and the life of a shipwrecked mariner is said to be little regarded if it be an obstacle to its gratification.'

However, he put in to Kárystos, in spite of its being 'a place of such evil repute, and so little frequented'.[1]

But it was mainly the pirates who made the channel and its surroundings so dreaded by sailors. As a result of Licario's descent upon the islands in about 1285, the number of pirates greatly increased, and this coast of Euboea continued to be a favourite lurking place for them until well into the nineteenth century. Dr Sibthorp, on that same voyage in 1794, was nearly as closely beset by pirates as by dolphins: there were rumours of them everywhere. He had scarcely left Negroponte, and was sailing between the Attic coast and the island of Macronisi, when 'A small boat came off from the latter with some goatherds, who informed us, that the preceding day a corsair had taken a great vessel: our captain's eyes now pierced every creek; and a considerable alarm arose on seeing two small vessels in the port of Therico '.²

As late as the year 1844 nine cases of piracy were reported in the course of a few months in these waters, in which nearly all those on board the captured ships were murdered. In the same year *The Times* reported that 'Letters from Athens announce that some pirate boats in the Channel of Andros had captured two merchant vessels—one a royal cutter with four men and carrying 16,000 drachmas belonging to the Greek Government —and put their crews to death. The headless bodies of twenty of the pirates' victims were washed ashore on the coast of Andros'.³

There were occasions, however, when the pirates proved less formidable, if one may judge from the experience of Mr Cockerell, who, in 1810, was sailing by the Sporades in a Greek merchantman bound for Salonica. 'Off Scopolo,' he writes, 'a boat came out and fired a gun at us to heave to. The crew told me she was a pirate, but when we fired again in return to show that we also were armed, the crew of the boat merely wished us a happy journey!' ⁴ There is something rather engaging in these pirates, who, in spite of their disappointment, did not forget their manners! They might in fact have hailed from Penzance:

> Although our dark career
> Sometimes involves the crime of stealing,
> We rather think that we're
> Not altogether void of feeling.

Gavrion is on the west coast of Andros, and coming to it from Kárystos, we did not enter the Doro channel; but we hugged Euboea for some distance, and it certainly is an unpleasant coastline for a shipwreck, rocky and steep-to, with nothing much apparent in the way of sheltered inlets. But nowadays it is not the pirates but Poseidon who is apt to deter folk from coming this way, for it has the reputation of being a stormy passage: the current runs strongly, while, as

Mr Hawkins noted, the north wind seems to be funnelled down with particular violence from the mountains round Kárystos.

But on this occasion the sea was glassy, and nowhere among all these rocks did it so much as bare a tooth. We came into Gavrion just as the light was beginning to fade: a jutting pyramid of rock guarded the entrance, and behind, the long black Saranda ridge coiled like a watching dragon round the bay and the little white nest of a town.

Debarkation into a rowing-boat was accompanied with the usual outcry. There was quite a crowd of us, and, as always on these occasions, creeping into a strange shore, as outsiders amid a genial group of locals, we felt a trifle forlorn.

About an hour and a quarter by bus brought us to Port Andros on the other side of the island, where we set about finding an hotel. It was not so easy. We asked for the 'Paradissos': no-one had heard of it, but everyone had a conviction it was an unattainable as its name implied. It would be closed. For certain. We mentioned the 'Triton'. Ah, that was definitely closed. A French-speaking woman very kindly told us she would take us to a room in a private house; but I am always unwilling to do this if it can be avoided. One is not so free; and, in my experience, the beds are more likely to be hard! Of course the odds are always on the beds being hard in Greece; nor, unlike the beds of France and Germany, are they wont to have their hardness alleviated by several mattresses. Without doubt this is a paltry consideration not to be weighed by any traveller worthy of the name, especially if he remembers the gallant example of those earlier visitors to Greece who suffered with equanimity such appalling discomfort; but I cannot pretend that I am indifferent to it. Eventually, an obliging fellow led us to a small hotel in the town. It was clean and pleasant, and the beds might have been worse.

We dined at a restaurant in the main street, and afterwards went out to explore the town by moonlight, with the object of finding the tower that is the last relic of the castle built about 1207 by Marino Dandolo, a nephew of the old Doge.

In a minute or two we again met the French-speaking woman, who told us she knew the island well, and would be glad to take us round next day. I asked her the way to Marino's tower, but to my amazement she told me flatly there was nothing of the kind in the town. I find this incredible. Had she, unlike James James' mother, never gone down to the end of the town! That would be even more remarkable than the case of the farmer and his wife, encountered by Mr Bradford on Kythnos, who lived within six miles of the sea, and had never been to it.[5] As diplomatically as I could, I declined her offer.

Andros, that night, was very peaceful, and very dark: everyone was indoors, even the cafés appeared to have closed early, and we had the streets almost to ourselves. They were badly lighted, but fortunately there was a moon, aided by which we wondered through the lanes, knowing nothing of the topography, and continually finding ourselves brought to the edge of the sea. There was no sign of a tower. So quiet and empty was the town, that it might have been a deserted film lot, with façades that had nothing and no-one behind them; but then I noticed that although there wasn't a sound there was movement—a swift gliding of small creatures in the shadows. For a horrid moment I imagined rats.

'Cats!' exclaimed Aileen, who had noticed them at the same moment.

I do not think I have ever encountered so many cats at one time. It reminded me of the Algernon Blackwood story in which, on a certain night, all the inhabitants of a village were wont to turn into cats, and attend their local witches to a coven. Whether or not the Andros cats were bound for a coven, they definitely struck us as a dour, businesslike lot of go-getters, with no time for philandering—at least if one might judge by the absence of any serenade. The fact being that, like the majority of their kind in Greece, they were hungry, and after food rather than love.

We came quite suddenly on our objective. At the extreme point of the promontory, beyond a narrow channel, rose a great bastion of rock, on top of which Marino's tower showed up dominant and black against the luminous sky. A single fragile arch curved over the channel, and made a precarious bridge. (Plate IV) That night we went no farther.

Herodotus tells us that the Greek fleet, pursuing the Persians after Salamis, put in to Andros. Themistocles endeavoured to raise money from the inhabitants, pointing out that he was supported by two powerful deities, Persuasion and Necessity; but the Andrians refused, explaining that they also had two deities, Poverty and Impossibility, who forbade it.[6] The Crusaders, on their way to the capture of Constantinople, called at Andros, and Geoffrey de Villehardouin writes in his Chronicle that 'The knights took their arms, and over-rode the country',[7] a grimly suggestive phrase. Later, when Marco Sanudo set out to conquer the Greek islands of the Archipelago, he had as one of his companions, Marino Dandolo, who succeeded in capturing Andros, which he held as a fief of the Duchy.

On Marino's death without heirs, there was trouble. Half the island went to the widow, the Lady of Andros, and half was bestowed by the second Duke on a Ghisi; but the unscrupulous Ghisi seized the whole. The Lady, however, was not defeated: she cast round for a champion with influence, and having found one in Jacopo Quirini of Astypalea, she engaged his interest, in more ways than one, by marrying him; and the two appealed to Venice. But each side could pull strings there, and the result was a deadlock that lasted until Ghisi, the Lady, and the Duke were all dead. After which, Andros was quietly taken over by the third Duke of Naxos, who diplomatically made a small payment to the Quirini's son, who turned up at the last minute to make a claim.

A hundred years later, another Lady of Andros suffered a similar injustice. She was Maria Sanudo, the daughter, by a second marriage, of the charming Duchess Fiorenza, who had inherited the Duchy, and had subsequently been the heroine of a very picturesque romance. Maria had received Andros as a gift from her father; then her parents died, the next Duke, her

half-brother, was murdered, and was succeeded in 1383 by
the man responsible for the crime, Francesco Crispo—who
promptly deprived Maria of Andros.

The reason was entirely diplomatic : as an usurper with the
taint of murder clinging to him, Crispo badly needed friends
and backers, and by bestowing Andros on Pietro Zeno, the
son of the Venetian Bailie of Negroponte, he obtained a powerful ally. He gave Maria, as compensation, Paros, on condition
that she married a certain Gasparo di Sommaripa: another
astute move, for the Sommaripa at that date were 'nobodies'
in this aristocratic and extremely exclusive island world, and
Crispo hoped that such a misalliance would detract from
Maria's influence. She was always a potential danger, since she
had a claim not only to Andros, but also to the dukedom. Maria
had to agree, and to marry Sommaripa, but, with all the
obstinacy of the Sanudi, she never gave up her claim to Andros;
and a day was to come when its justice would be recognized.

Pietro Zeno, the new ruler of Andros, was one of the most
famous diplomats of the age. The fact reminds one that, in
the words of William Miller, 'the baronies of the Archipelago
became a school for the governors and diplomatists whom the
republic of St Mark required in the Levant, and it was thence
that she often selected her bailies of Negroponte and her
captains of Modon and Koron'.[8] Incidentally, Zeno makes a
link with England; for in 1404 he went there to ask the aid
of Henry IV against the Ottoman Turks, who were then
threatening to overwhelm the Duchy. On another occasion,
when Henry Beaufort, Bishop of Winchester, the uncle, friend
and late chancellor of Henry V, was on pilgrimage to Palestine,
he was brought back to Venice on one of Zeno's galleys.[9]

Pietro's son and successor, Andrea, died in 1437, leaving an
only daughter. Venice, who had long had her eye on Andros,
at once endeavoured to seize it; but she was forestalled. The
Duke at this time was a minor, but his uncles stepped in,
imprisoned Andrea's widow in the old castle at Andros, and
tried to compel her agreement to a marriage between her

daughter and the young Duke. Venice was furious. She immediately brought such pressure to bear that the Duchy was forced to withdraw, and Andros was ruled by the Republic for the next three years.

During this time all the claimants to the island came to Venice to plead their cases, and at the end of the three years, in 1440, Andros was awarded to Maria Sanudo's son, Crusino I Sommaripa, who was Lord of Paros, and a triarch of Euboea. Thus, after more than fifty years, justice was done.

The Sommaripa held Andros until, early in the sixteenth century, it was captured by Barbarossa, and although it was returned to the Sommaripa, they lost it in 1566 by a revolution of the people. The last Sommaripa fled; the last Lady of Andros, accompanied by her brother, the last Frankish Duke of Naxos, took refuge in the Morea; and the Turk reigned supreme.

A final glimpse of Andros under Turkish rule, at the outset of the eighteenth century, is afforded by Tournefort—that learned, inquisitive, gossipy French botanist who toured the Aegean at this time. Andros was still the seat of a Latin bishop, and Tournefort writes:

> 'The Latin Bishop has but 300 crowns a year. Some time ago a sad Accident befell him: as he was passing from Andros to Naxia, the place of his Birth, with his Robes and Church-plate, he was taken by the Turks, stript, bastinado'd, put in the Gallies, and was fain to pay 500 Crowns for his Deliverance: he never could discover the least colour of reason for their serving him so.' [10]

Some twelve miles south of Port Andros, in the hills above Korthion, there is a castle known as the Apanocastro, or Upper Castle, and we were anxious to get to it; but first we had to know when and how we could go on from Andros to our next island, Tenos.

'I'll find out,' I said to Aileen the next morning, achieving a note of nonchalant confidence, but inwardly contemplating a familiar ordeal without much enthusiasm. I had recourse to the porter-and-general-attendant at our hotel: he had only a few words of English, but he was a willing, intelligent fellow and I thought we might reach an understanding. Our conversation took the routine course. I asked him in my best Greek when we could get to Tenos. He replied with a flow of Greek from which I emerged clinging desperately to a single word: Kyriakí, which means 'Sunday'.

'Well,' I said to Aileen, hoping I was right, 'the key fact seems to be that today is Sunday.'

He took valiantly to his English. 'Nothing,' he said, shaking his head. 'No. Nothing. Tomorrow.'

'We must make our arrangements tomorrow,' I interpreted.

'But what arrangements?' asked Aileen, with awkward persistence.

I ran an eye over the thin ranks of my Greek vocabulary, selected one or two for the forlorn hope, and advanced once more.

This time we seemed to get nowhere, and my courage faltered a little.

'Wait!' he exclaimed, and hurried from the room, to return presently with another Greek. The newcomer approached me with a smile.

'How do you do?' he said. 'How are you? How can I help?'

This sounded magnificent; and I launched at once into an inquiry as to when there would be a boat for Tenos, and what means there were, beforehand, of getting to the Apanocastro. In a matter of moments, however, I saw a glazed look come into his eyes. I stopped; and repeated the first question laboriously in Greek; his face lit up; he burst into speech—and it was my eyes that turned glassy. It was no use, we both had the questions, but there seemed no prospect of our obtaining the answers.

'How do you do?' he began again. 'How are you? How long do you stay?'

Somehow I managed to convey that there was really no future in our cross-talk, and presently we parted with a complete lack of understanding, but radiant smiles.

I stood up for another round with the porter. I don't know how long it took, but in the end, with a great expenditure of nods, shakes, eyebrow lifting, and arm waving, interspersed with graphic miming of driving a car, and of a small boat rocking in a swell, we achieved a measure of comprehension. I learnt that there would be a local boat running to Korthion tomorrow, and that another, connecting with this, would cross from Korthion to Tenos. As for the Apanocastro, there was a public taxi service to Korthion most days, but not on Sundays. A taxi to Korthion and back today would cost 300 drachmae, and was, we felt, too much.

While I was recuperating after this trying effort, the porter found another Greek, staying in the hotel, who really knew a little English, and I was able to confirm that a boat would be leaving about two o'clock next day for Korthion. Aileen and I talked it over, and decided that we would set out at once for the Apanocastro, and try to reach it on foot; this would give us the next morning to visit Marino's tower.

We got away about 10.30, and marched south in blazing sunshine, into the hills. The path went over a high bluff, and then along the brow of a deep gorge that ran for several miles towards a ridge. It was hard going, for the track, narrow and stony between low drystone walls, was composed mainly of an interminable succession of *skáles*, or staircases, built up, or cut in the rock, on the hillside. Up and down and round the mountain went these steps; there was little shade on the bare, burnt-up hills, and the experience was as wearisome as a treadmill. Even Aileen, who normally tittups over rock as lightly as an oread, dragged a bit.

After an hour or so we came to the village of Sineti, which was strewn precariously, like a fall of white rock, on the lip of the gorge, about a thousand feet above the valley floor. As we trailed through the village, we were hailed by an Americano from his house by the wayside, and invited in. Grateful for the respite, we sat for a few minutes, chatting and drinking cherry jam dissolved in water, which was delicious; our host, whose name was Miltiades, delighting to air his excellent English, told us of his years in the States—while his wife and his sisters and his children gathered round to look benevolently, but with incredulity, upon people who walked the mountains in the heat of the day from choice!

Sineti claws to the hillside wherever it can manage to get a hold, which isn't everywhere, and the result is a village through which, small as it is, it is difficult for a stranger to find his way. To get out of it, one has to go up or down from level to level, by inconspicuous *skáles*, until, like a ship in a lock, one arrives at the correct level for exit. There is nothing, however, to indicate when this stage is reached, and we were grateful to Miltiades' sister who very kindly guided us to the main track. She left us with a wave of her hand towards the path ahead and the terse comment: '*Skáles! Skáles! Skáles!*'

How right she was! Up and down, up and down, we went, and still the gorge wound ahead. We clumped on, and sweated —occasionally in doubt about the way, when other lanes branched off, each flanked by neat drystone walls. These were beautifully built of stone chipped flat, and arranged in a pattern not unlike that of a military parapet, for, at intervals of a few feet, a large stone would be set in the wall parallel to the road, which gave the appearance of a row of blind embrasures; and, in between *skáles*, stumbling through this maze of narrow, parapeted tracks that wound over bare, scorched earth, one might have imagined one was in a communication trench of the First World War!

At length we neared the head of the gorge, where its floor began to ascend. Our path dropped to it, and we crossed by a stone bridge to the opposite cliff, and began to mount the *skáles* that would bring us over the col at the end. Just here, we met with what in a Greek summer is practically a miracle —a trickle of water spilling down the arid hillside into a tiny rock pool. It was an ecstatic meeting, which delayed us more than a little. Eventually, after we had been walking between four and five hours, we topped the ridge and there, two or three miles ahead, jauntily poised on a low hill, was our castle.

Alas, it was too far. We didn't fancy negotiating the *skáles* in the dark, but if we were to make Port Andros by nightfall, we must turn back; and so, despondently, we gave it up.

It was 6.30, and dark, when we reached our hotel; and eight hours of *skáles* in that sweltering heat had made quite a gruelling day.

The next morning we went down to Marino's tower.

Andros is one of the prettiest towns in the islands. The older part is built on a tongue of rock thrust into the bay, so that it has the sea on three sides; and its narrow cross-lanes, with jutting balconies and splashes of bloom over white garden walls, drop down to a glitter of blue water. Only mules and donkeys share the lanes with pedestrians, and it is a quiet place, except when the wind blows, and it fills with the thunder of the sea, as though it were a great ship driving into the bay. (Plate III)

We found the bridge not nearly as difficult to cross as it looked. The flat-topped cliff on which the tower stands continues the line of the town promontory, and runs for about one hundred and fifty yards in a north-easterly direction; the tower is at the western edge, on a small rocky platform, sixty yards from the bridge. Built of greenish stone, with immensely thick walls, it rises to about thirty feet, with an entrance on the west, and a chamber inside some sixteen feet by ten, with a vaulted roof. It exhibits no cavities nor breaches, the surface has merely crumbled under the elements of seven and a half centuries, and the tower has weathered as though it were a solid mass of masonry, or part of the crag itself that has been roughly hewn. The effect is of great strength; indeed, viewed from the land, this shaggy old watchdog, held in leash by the delicate loop of the bridge, still has a defiant air.

On at least one occasion, however, it proved a poor guard; for here, one night in the late seventeenth century, pirate galleys, commanded by the famous French corsair, Hugues Creveliers, quietly anchored, and before morning their crews had well and truly pillaged Andros. Creveliers, who is said to have been the original of Byron's 'Corsair', dominated the Aegean for several years, and made such a good thing out of it that he was about to retire on his booty, when a vindictive servant blew him up in his flagship.[11]

At the north-eastern end of the cliff there are the remains of a square bastion in a very ruinous condition, which also has a small vaulted chamber, with an embrasure opening seawards. Plainly the original castle consisted of the tower, or keep, from which the wall of the single enceinte ran round the perimeter of the cliff, through the sea bastion, and through other outworks that have now vanished. It would, I thought, have been a disturbing eyrie in which to live, clamorous with wind and sea, and, in time of storm, haunted by the bellowing of water churning in the narrow gut.

Patches of the hottentot fig, better known as mesembry-anthemum, or, down Cornwall way, as Sally-my-handsome, grew on the cliff, showing green, fleshy leaves but no flowers; elsewhere, the grass grew lank and brown, and hid one more martial relic, the barrel of an ancient cannon.

Coming down to the bridge from the tower, one has a view over the whole town, a tight cluster of houses clinging to this narrow raft of land—with the life of its people not inaptly symbolized by the statue, at this end, of a sailor, his ditty-bag over his shoulder, his face towards the sea, and his hand raised in farewell. For so many of the island folk are, or have been, sailors; and directly one hears a man speaking a few words of English, one may safely deduce that he picked them up in Liverpool—it is nearly always Liverpool—while his ship was in port.

It was blowing quite hard while we were on the rock, and back at the hotel our Greek friend told us it was too rough for the local boats to run. He added, however, that there would be a boat from the Piraeus to Tenos, which would call at Port Andros, and after that at Korthion, where it would arrive at 6.30. We decided to take it, and in the meantime to make another effort to reach the Apanocastro, and get down to Korthion in time to catch the boat.

The most likely means was the public taxi service, which, this being Monday, was now in operation, and which charged the moderate sum of fifty drachmae per person for the drive to Korthion. We sallied out to make inquiries, but found no-one able to tell us anything, and it seemed to us the taxi service was conducted with a secrecy worthy of an underground movement! At this juncture we met a woman cousin of our Greek friend, who spoke English better than he did, and who charitably took the affair in hand. She led us out to the *platea* and eventually found a man, who declared the service was booked up for that day. He suggested we should take mules.

There is always something exhilarating in the prospect of mules—offering its illusion of escape from pampered wafting to honest travel! It is an illusion for which, as we well know, one has to pay dearly in discomfort; nevertheless, Aileen longs for a mule as Richard longed for a horse, and feels that only on mule-back has she really achieved true romance, and joined the ancient brotherhood of genuine travellers. Secretly, I feel much the same. No doubt to fly in a plane is just as romantic as the Roc's progress of Sindbad, but it lacks the glamour that accumulates with legend and tradition.

So we settled for mules; and the porter produced them with the ease that a conjurer produces rabbits. In twenty minutes they appeared in front of the hotel. Our lady explained to the muleteer that we wanted to go to the Apanocastro first, where we should spend at least half an hour before going down to Korthion. He smiled, and we certainly thought he had understood. Later, I was to wonder whether he had not, or whether it was simply that in Greece, as in Denmark, a man may smile, and smile, and be a villain!

We mounted. It was not as easy as it sounds; and once up we were horribly uncomfortable. Edward Lear complained long ago that Greek saddles were appalling, and they have not improved since then: they are really pack saddles, with horizontal wooden slats, and not only does one writhe miserably on this gridiron, but, since it is impossible to get a fair grip on it with one's legs, one teeters like an untied bale. We had once made a long journey on mules to the Styx, and fancied we knew all the horrors; but this ride was worse, for now each mule carried a suitcase as well, which meant that the rider's leg on that side was forced up on the animal's neck, and even the attempt at a grip had to be abandoned.

We started at midday, seen off by our kind, but, I have no doubt, greatly relieved helpers, to whom, I fear, we had been an unmitigated nuisance. The muleteer took, of course, our track of yesterday, and in a short time we reached the *skáles*. The mules clambered up and down with nonchalant ability, toppling us backward and forward, bouncing us up and catching us in a game of cup-and-ball that, to judge by their bored indifference, was a game they had played too often with tourists.

'I think—I'd—sooner—walk!' gasped Aileen, and I agreed. Nor did the muleteer help matters. No sooner did we settle down to a kind of shuttlecock rhythm, than he would let out a piercing screech, welt the nearest mule with his stick, and goad the brute to sudden frantic exertions that shook one until the bones began to rattle in one's carcase like spillikins in a bag.

Four hours of this; and then at last our castle showed up on the horizon. A few moments later, to my utter dismay, our muleteer directed the animals down a lane that led away from the castle.

'Wait!' I exclaimed, pulling up, and pointing to the castle. 'Apanocastro!'

He shook his head, and pointed to Korthion.

I expostulated—my Greek more barbaric than ever from emotion. He replied at length. I gathered there was no time to get to the castle and then down to the boat. Perhaps he was right; but I felt he had known perfectly well that we wanted to visit the castle, and he had made no difficulty about the time. I concluded he had never had any intention of going as far as the castle, and had simply taken advantage of us. I was very angry—but there was little I could do, with our luggage as a hostage on his mules!

He was determined not to go to the castle; so I tried to get him to carry the luggage to Korthion, while we went to the castle on foot, and met him later in the town; but he either would not or could not understand. Looking round in desperation, I noticed a man working in a field, and went across to him on the faint chance that he might speak English. He didn't, and I turned back—leaving him charmed by what he evidently imagined was a friendly greeting in passing!

'You go on with the luggage,' I said to Aileen, 'and I'll sprint up to the castle, take a few photographs, and be down before the boat sails.'

'No,' she replied firmly. 'I will never desert Mr Micawber! If you go, I go.'

We hesitated; but we were certainly very anxious to catch that boat; and it hardly seemed wise to leave the luggage with a disgruntled muleteer—so in the end we capitulated.

We took a last look at the castle that had twice defied us. Sullenly, I mounted my mule. The muleteer gave a yell that seemed to ring with derisive triumph; the mules waggled their ears in ironic understanding; and we wobbled sadly down the *skáles* to Korthion.

66

Plate I EUBOEA. *Castel Rosso, north wall* ▷

△ Plate II EUBOEA. *Kárystos. Castel Rosso in background*

▽ Plate III ANDROS. *Andros Town*

△ Plate IV ANDROS. *Marino's Tower*

△ Plate V TENOS. *Exobourgo*

△ Plate VI SYRA. *Platea Miaoulis*

△ Plate VII NAXOS. *Citadel. Main Gate*

△ Plate VIII NAXOS. *Citadel. Tower*

Chapter Five

TENOS: Last Stronghold
SYRA: War of the Ass

KORTHION is small and quiet, but it has an hotel, and is a pleasant place to stay, if one doesn't mind being elbowed by mountains at every turn; for at Korthion one is trapped, like an insect at the bottom of a cup, and, apart from the sea, there is no way out except by a strenuous climb.

Our boat—the *Despina*—came at the end of an hour and a half; so I reckoned we should in fact probably have had time to do the castle. In spite of our only having 'deck' tickets, the agent, embarrassingly, treated us as distinguished foreigners, and having beckoned us out of the waiting crowd, took us aboard in his launch.

The sun had now set, and there was quite a chill in the air, so we went down to the lower, covered deck. It was fairly full. Among the passengers was an elderly Englishman with an untidy white beard, wearing a shirt, plus-fours, shoes and no stockings. I had seen him before, wandering about Andros town in a kind of impatient abstraction—the air of a man who had no interest whatever in his immediate environment, but whose eye was fixed on an ultimate, invisible goal. I knew he was English, because he had come to our hotel to make an inquiry of the porter. Now he had the same aura of aloofness, the same manner of looking through the scene about him; and I didn't venture to speak to him.

But I fancied that the detachment, the inward turning gaze, betokened the recluse, who prefers his own company, and I

67

◁ Plate IX NAXOS, *Apeiranthos*

toyed with the notion that he was an anchorite returning to a retreat in the Aegean. To some remote and abandoned but by no means ruinous monastery, of which there are many in the islands, where a solitary might make himself reasonably comfortable—I knew at least of one such hermit, who had lived for many years in the small deserted monastery on the top of Mount Ithome. Looking at those plus-fours, so long out of fashion, so very ancient, I deduced that their wearer had already spent years in his retreat; and now, having been temporarily recalled to the world by urgent and unavoidable business, he was returning to his cell with the concentration of a homing pigeon. It was a fable that afforded me much satisfaction!

Another passenger was a young Greek, lame and evidently a very sick man, who lay stretched out on one of the slatted wooden benches. He was travelling with his sister, and they, like ourselves, were going to Tenos, where it was probable he hoped to obtain his healing from the famous wonder-working ikon in the church of Panayia Evangelistria. This ikon was discovered in 1822, and now, twice a year, on March 25th and August 15th, it draws a great crowd of pilgrims, among whom are many invalids seeking a cure. Cures are certainly made; and Tenos has become the holy island of the Greek orthodox world, as Delos was of ancient Greece. There is, too, another link with the practice of classical Greece; for here the patient often follows the procedure in the healing sanctuaries of Asclepius, and sleeps in the precinct.

The island is also, unexpectedly, the seat of a Catholic bishop, and has a strong Catholic element. The shrine is of course a very profitable affair for the islanders; and it would have been another miracle to the credit of the ikon if Tenos had altogether avoided the commercialism that inevitably gathers, as it has always done, round these pilgrim centres. As one outcome of this, Tenos is accustomed to welcoming visitors, and is a good island on which to stay 'out of season'.

Two hours brought us to the town and port of Tenos, on the south-west of the island: it is a large and well-sheltered harbour, deep enough, we were glad to find, for boats to come alongside the quay. We booked in at an hotel on the front, and then, because our hotel, as is usual outside Athens, had no restaurant, we walked out to obtain a meal, and to reconnoitre the town.

Latin Tenos came into being in 1207, when the island was taken by the Ghisi, in which family it remained until 1390. Then, together with Mykonos and Delos, it passed by will to Venice. The rule of Venice was popular in the islands, so far as any foreign rule could be, and the islanders, at a time when they feared the Republic might give up Tenos, declared they would emigrate sooner than be handed to another master, and that 'No lordship under heaven is as just and good as that of Venice'.[1]

Venice did not indeed want the bother of running the island, and in the archives of the Senate is an announcement, dated 16th June 1391, which reads: 'Notice to the inhabitants of Crete, of Coron, Modon, Venetians, friends or subjects, that in the month of December, at Venice, there will be sold to the highest bidder the islands of Tenos and Mykonos; the price will be payable over ten years.'[2] It was hardly a very attractive bargain: Tenos and Mykonos had never fully recovered from the ravages of the Spanish admiral, Roger de Lluria, at the end of the thirteenth century; Turkish pirates had descended on them since, and Delos, also included in the sale, was merely a rendezvous for these pirates. However, in actual fact, Venice intended to sell no more than a four-year lease of the islands to one of her nobles, who would be under the authority of the Venetian Bailie of Euboea; and on these terms she found a purchaser.

Tenos next ran some risk of becoming entirely deserted; for in 1413 Giovanni Quirini, lord of Astypalaia, who was then governing Tenos and Mykonos, began deporting the people to repopulate his own island of Astypalaia, which had suffered badly from Turkish raids. This forced migration, however, raised an uproar; Venice immediately objected, and Quirini was compelled to return the people to their home. Soon afterwards, Venice acceded to the wishes of the inhabitants of Tenos and Mykonos, and took direct charge of these islands, appointing a *provveditore*, or rector, who was independent of the Bailie of Euboea.

On the whole, Venetian rule was beneficial to Tenos; but although the island was given some protection by the fleet of the Republic, for which many islanders were conscripted, the Turkish raids still continued, and long before the end of the fifteenth century the Turks were indeed paramount in the Aegean. All had fallen to them, Greece and the Byzantine Empire—Constantinople, Athens, the Morea—while the Duke of Naxos and the remaining Latin dynasties in the Archipelago existed only by the Sultan's goodwill, which was procured by the payment of tribute. What happened when this goodwill was withdrawn was shown in 1537, when Barbarossa made his savage attack upon the Cyclades.

He desolated island after island.

'In each of the islands that he took, he began by killing all the Catholics; among the Greeks, he slaughtered the old men; took the young men to row in his galleys, sent the children to Constantinople to swell the corps of janissaries; as to the women, he ordered them to dance before him and kept for his harem those that pleased him. After him, his officers made their choice one after the other, according to their rank, and the ugliest women were left to the common sailors.'[3]

Mykonos was lost; and Tenos surrendered at once, handing over its *provveditore* to Barbarossa. Then, however, the people had a change of heart: they hoisted the banner of St Mark again, sent for aid to Crete, and with the help of these reinforcements, held the island for Venice.

Thirty years later the Sultan took over the Archipelago,

imprisoned the last Crispi Duke, and the islands fell, 'as plates dropp'd from his pocket', into the lap of his Jewish favourite, Joseph Nasi. There remained to the Latins only Tenos, and in addition Siphnos, with six lesser islands, where the Gozzadini were restored as puppets of the Sultan. But it was whispered to the Sultan that the garden of the Cyclades 'is all your majesty's, save this one tree, which is Tenos'; and accordingly another attempt was made on Tenos by the Turks under Piali Pasha, an Hungarian renegade.

The island, with its nearly impregnable fortress of Exobourgo, was defended with great courage by its *provveditore*, Girolamo Paruta, and the Turks were driven off. Three years later they tried once more, with no better success; and thereafter no serious attack was made on it for over a hundred and forty years. In 1617 the Gozzadini were swept away, and the Crescent floated over all the Latin possessions in the Aegean save one— Tenos still defied the Turk, and Exobourgo still flew the banner of St Mark.

It was of course the strength of this fortress that enabled Tenos to hold out for so long; yet Venice neglected it shamefully. Tournefort, visiting the island in 1700, remarked of Exobourgo: 'The Fortress of Tenos is on a Rock that overlooks the Country, and is stronger by Nature than Art: the Guard of it is committed to fourteen shabby Soldiers, seven of them are French Deserters'. Exobourgo was, even in the later years, the only safe place on the island, and, says Tournefort, 'The best People of the Island dwell here, tho' there are not above 500 Houses, which are much incommoded by the North-wind, as cutting as at Paris'. He adds that in Venice they look on the *provveditore's* post as a 'Place of mortification'.[4]

That was certainly, one fancies, how the last *provveditore*, Bernard Balbi, looked upon it. For when another Turco-Venetian war broke out in 1714, Tenos was attacked, and Balbi gave up the island without a struggle. He marched out, presumably at the head of his fourteen veterans, with all the honours of war—leaving the wretched inhabitants to be enslaved. Not unreasonably, Venice was shocked, and imprisoned him for life.

Even in modern times Tenos has not been immune from lawless and piratical attacks. On 15th August 1940 the island was full of pilgrims celebrating the great annual Feast of the Assumption, and in the harbour, decked with flags in honour of the occasion, was anchored the light cruiser Elli. Greece was then at peace with the world; but at half-past eight in the morning the Elli was torpedoed by an Italian submarine, and an hour and a quarter later, she sank, one of her crew being killed, and twenty-nine injured.

Naturally, Exobourgo was our first objective on Tenos. The dome-shaped crest of rock on which it is built sticks up like a battered helmet on the horizon, and we could see it plainly from our hotel. It is only five or six miles away as the crow flies, and we decided to walk to it, taking the short cut by a mule track at the west end of the town, which mounts over the hills in a long trail of skáles. An hour and a half of toiling up the steps under a torrid sun brought us over the ridge, and another half hour took us to the village of Kinara at the foot of Exobourgo.

Kinara is the residence of a Catholic bishop, and perhaps from the necessity of living up to this, or because of the episcopal eye, it is the most immaculate of villages, with a pervading air of spit and polish that would do justice to a military cantonment on the eve of a general's inspection. At the entrance to it a tree or two provides welcome shade, beyond which the village shines naked in the sun, as white and spotless as the lawn of a bishop's sleeve. Over it looms the enormous rounded crag of Exobourgo, a petrified wave 1,700 feet high, on which are the ruins of the Venetian citadel. (Plate V) At the moment the side facing us was in shadow, and it was not until we saw it in the sun that we realized the rock, owing to the lichen on it, is the colour of gold.

We found a French-speaking Greek woman, who ran a tiny

shop in the main street, where we were able to slake our now considerable thirst with lemonade. She directed us to the Exobourgo track, a lane that leads off from the far end of the village, and winds round the south and east of the rock, gradually ascending to the summit.

Underfoot the track is a rickle of stones, usable now only by pedestrians and mules. Stumbling along it, we came presently to the south-east face of the crag, and into the sun pouring down furiously and beating off the blazing rock that rose almost sheer to our left, so that we seemed to be melting in a golden crucible. At the foot of the rock where there had once been houses, there was nothing left but loose stones, until, a short distance on, appeared the remains of what was probably the town wall, and here one could trace the ground plan of a line of buildings. Pushing on and up, we found the rock taking an easier slope, and presently were able to see above us a bastion and wall belonging to the outer defences of the fortress proper. At the point where the path reached this wall, there was another redoubt, preceded by a breach that may have been the site of an outer gate of the citadel.

Farther on, as we later found, there is, within the enceinte, an intriguing underground gallery that branches, one arm leading to an open embrasure, and the other to what may have been a sally-port that emerges in a crack in the cliff face; but the main way goes through the breach, and winds over the enceinte to where there are the massive ruins of a tower and a stretch of the inner curtain. Climbing steeply, it crosses the curtain at what was presumably the second gate, of which there is nothing left now, and reaches a third and last gate above, which gives access to the inmost enclosure, the summit of the crag. Here no doubt there was once a keep, but today it is occupied only by a large stone cross.

All these remains are on the east and north-east side of the rock; on the north-west there is another fine stretch of wall, which appears to have contained a second outer gate, and which has at its western end a tiny chapel perched on the top of the precipice. From west round to south-east the rock falls sheer, and there was no need for fortifications.

That is about all there is, except for a few cisterns, one beside the west gate, and an arcade of five arches within the highest enceinte, which may have carried a length of curtain. From such blurred and broken fragments, one can really only guess at the details of the fortress's lay-out. As for the town that once clustered within these walls, it has left only a sprinkling of stones, unless one includes the ruins of the little Frankish church, far down below to the north-east, which must certainly have lain outside the boundary.

The rock has shaken off its human limpets, and what remains of their work it has encrusted with its lichen and fused with itself, to emerge once more as a thing of beauty in its own right. It assuredly is that. At the foot of the crag, between it and the Frankish church, are the dazzling white buildings of a modern monastery, and if one looks from the church to the monastery against its background of glowing rock, the scene has a barbaric splendour, as of some chryselephantine carving, in ivory and gold. But it is not only its beauty that makes it fascinating, but also its odd reserve; for it is loath to remind you of its past. Much drama has been played here, and yet, for all the fragments of the citadel, it is difficult to call it up. One is continually feeling that in a moment everything will take shape in one's mind, that one will see the mounting concentric fortifications with their great towers and redoubts, and the huddled terraces of houses piled one above another; that one will get the atmosphere of this forlorn outpost, so utterly alone, with its watcher for ever anxiously scrutinizing every galley that bore towards the island. But no, the rock offers you no co-operation; it glows in the sun and demands your admiration, but as for the past, when men disfigured it, it is doing all it can to obliterate the traces of that.

It surprises me that the fortress remained impregnable; for the approach on the north-east is not, so far as natural obstacles are concerned, very difficult, and one remembers how really fantastic eyries like the Palamedi at Nauplia have been taken by storm. Yet it must have proved tough to keep out Barbarossa.

From the top one can see all the Cyclades, and it is held that on a very clear day the Sporades are visible; but now we found that even the western Cyclades were but a blur on the horizon.

We stayed up there until late afternoon, enjoying a faint waft of Tournefort's hated north wind. Apart from a Catholic priest climbing up to the monastery on a mule, we met no-one, and had the rock to ourselves, except for a pair of ravens, one or two hawks, a number of jackdaws and a rout of red admiral butterflies. Looking in at the neglected little Frankish church, we found the south wall had gone, but that parts of the other three remained, with pillars at the east and west ends, bearing a modified acanthus leaf on their capitals, that supported ribs and broken bits of a vaulted roof. The wild things flourished within: wallflowers, and knapweed that had grown into a great thorny ball that must have been a magnificent sight in bloom. Aileen lingered over this, for she has an especial fondness for the heavy-armed thistle, with his clean lines, and his bold front with levelled pikes, worthy of Socrates on the retreat from Delium, as Plato describes him, making it 'evident, even from afar, that whoever should venture to attack him would encounter a desperate resistance'. Here, of course, as in any Greek landscape, there was a fine phalanx of them— Scotch thistles in bloom, star thistles, and teasles, now withered; but the highlight for her was the discovery of a really superb milk thistle, whose yellow blooms are scented like mignonette, and whose parts once provided the Greeks with quite a varied dish, for its root was boiled, its leaves used as salad, and its head treated as an artichoke.

I think Aileen would have been content to camp out for the night in this happy hunting ground, but I was not tempted, and was prepared to remind her of Tournefort's experience in a similar place. 'These,' he says, 'are the Reflections we made at Joura in the night-time, as we lay in a ruinated Chapel, when we durst not sleep for fear the Field-mice should come and gnaw our Ears'! [4]

As it was, night fell while we were still on the *skáles* going home; but the moon was up, the landscape flooded with light, and looking back, we saw that the transmutation attempted by the alchemists had been performed in reverse, and that Exobourgo had turned from gold to silver.

The next morning, we walked over to Stavros bay, about three-quarters of a mile to the west of the town, a fascinating place, with little white chapels on the shore, which, as one comes down to the bay, stand out vividly against the blue water in a pattern as naïve as the country background in an Italian primitive. In the forefront of a low amphitheatre of hills at the head of the bay are the temples of Poseidon and his wife, Amphitrite. The ground plan of each temple is plain, there are the remains of two marble stoas, or exedras, and many marble blocks lie around, a number of them with inscriptions. The ruins are upon the shore, practically at sea level, and this, to my fancy, is more appropriate than if they were built on a cliff in the manner of the famous temple of Poseidon at Sunium. For surely the sea-god's temple should come as near as it can to mingling with the waves, so that the god may rise from his kingdom to the very threshold of his altar.

The old well with maidenhair fern lining its interior, which Scott O'Connor was charmed by in the nineteen-twenties, and mentioned with affection in his book *Isles of the Aegean*, was still there. With the water gleaming in that cool, dark grotto, the green spangles of fern drooping over it, and the opening canopied by a white poplar, the well, on this burning day, had an almost hypnotic appeal.

The following day we paid another visit to Exobourgo, making use of a bus that left at seven. Breakfast was brought to our room by the two chambermaids, who invariably appeared together—perhaps for mutual protection, since, whenever we encountered them, they fixed us with a doubtful, curious stare. 'For all the world,' said Aileen, 'like cows in a field as you pass!'

The bus, jolting horribly over an abominable road, took us to Kinara in about three-quarters of an hour, passing at a distance seven or eight little white villages, one lying in each fold of the hills, like a patch of unmelted snow. A Catholic priest, who sat beside us, in the bus, obligingly murmured their names, 'Kalamati, Kaloumenados . . .'. But more interesting to us were the medieval dovecotes, for which Tenos has always been noted: small square buildings with a pinnacle at each corner, they have a ground floor that is a room with solid walls, but above this, in the dovecote proper, the walls are built in peculiar lacy patterns full of interstices that allow the birds to pass in and out. Reminding one faintly of a doll's house, they look as quaint and exotic as the 'folly' in the grounds of an eighteenth-century eccentric.

Calling at the shipping office on the quay next day, we found that getting to Naxos, our immediate objective, would take us out of orbit, and that we must go first to Syra. So we booked on the evening boat, and strolled back along the quay to visit the Evangelistria, the church of the famous ikon.

Tenos, like Syra, is an exception to the usual run of Aegean ports that for most of the day, and some of them for days at a time, are as quiet as Lethe wharf, on whose weed-grown condition Hamlet's father reported. You may indeed hear the chug of an outboard motor now and then—and perhaps you can now hear that at Lethe wharf!—but apart from that there is little doing, save when the occasional caique drifts in or out, until the great moment when the Piraeus steamer condescends to heave-to in the offing. But in Tenos there is continual activity: steamers, yachts and caiques are coming or going, and seaplanes touch down in the harbour; there is no lack of bustle on the quay, and it is evident the holy island is equally to the fore in worldly matters.

For once, however, the quay was quiet, except for a man industriously beating an octopus on the stones to make it tender

—the octopus always looks very dead, but nevertheless it is a proceeding that seems to me horrid. I glanced away hurriedly, only to see another delusively barbarous spectacle, for a train of mules was passing laden with pigskin bags of wine, and as the whole hide is employed for a bag, the effect was that of a number of bloated corpses.

The Evangelistria is a modern building of a dazzling whiteness, with a three-tiered wedding-cake tower that lends it a pleasantly festive air, but it is hardly an architectural triumph. Yet one aspect I did find moving. For crouched at either side of the broad flight of steps leading up to the main entrance were two beggars: bowed, despondent forms in dark rags, firmly etched against that immaculate, shining portal, they might have been fallen humanity in despair before the gate of Paradise.

Beyond the entrance, on the right, is the best feature of the building, a noble court. Bounded on two sides by a double row of arches, one above the other, it has in the centre a fountain surmounted by a dove, about which stand four cypress trees, like four tall sentries in bearskins at a lying-in-state. Their towering dark plumage was a benediction to the eye amid the glare; but in a corner of the courtyard was a tree whose red blossoms had by contrast a quite outrageous flamboyance, as of scarlet and sinful blooms on the tree of knowledge in this shining Eden!

I had some difficulty in luring Aileen up the marble staircase that led to the body of the church.

'It's so lovely out here,' she said, following me reluctantly. 'But I'm not much taken with the interior of these Orthodox Byzantine churches—they're too dark, too fussy and littered with lamps and candle-holders and indifferent ikons. They haven't the sweep of line, and the spaciousness, that even a small Gothic church is able to convey.'

'Well, they're cosy,' I said; but I'm inclined to agree with her. The Evangelistria, however, turned out to be large, light and airy, but of course it was thick with votive offerings in silver, which hung from the roof, and had been presented in gratitude by those healed. It is customary to offer a representation of what has been cured, or of something connected with the healing or saving experience, so here were legs and arms and hearts and kidneys in silver, as well as a donkey, a house and ships of all kinds—among which was that famous offering, in gratitude for a miraculous preservation at sea, of a ship with a dolphin plugging a hole in the hull. The wonder-working ikon is kept below in the crypt, which covers the spot where it was found.

It was quiet in the church, with no-one there but a charwoman scrubbing the floor, and the peace and charm of the fountain court linger in the memory; but it must become a fearful place on the days of the great festivals, when many thousands of people converge upon it, and every nook and corner is jammed to suffocation. Theodore Bent has written of his experience on one of these occasions.

'Patience [he says], assisted now and again by an ingenious push, enabled us to get inside and witness the weird sights in the church—men and women were there grovelling on their knees; cripples, blind and halt, were imploring the favour of the Madonna; further on, a woman, after standing ominously still for a while, as if contemplating the scene, was suddenly seized by religious frenzy. She shrieked, she threw her arms about, and was carried out in wild hysteria. This frenzy was most infectious, and presently the whole church was full of hideous yells and maddened suppliants who are supposed when in this state to be under the special influence of the Deity . . . I could stand no more. Sick and faint, I reached the open air after a struggle with the pilgrims, who were eagerly pushing in with their little tin phials they had bought outside to fill with water from the sacred stream.' [5]

For our last meal in the restaurant they gave us koliós, a kind of mackerel, much better in my opinion than the famed barboúni, or red mullet, which is fairly riddled with bones; and to follow, as a gesture in recognition of our patronage, they presented us with a slice of melon 'on the house'.

The journey to Syra takes an hour and a half, and our boat, the old and shabby *Marilena*, pottered out at nightfall. We sat on the open upper deck under a gigantic moon, which, as the boat began to move, dropped out of a canopy of cloud and poised for a moment on the masthead like a ball of St Elmo's fire. Under its radiance the little white town glistened as though it had risen, at the word of Poseidon, from the depth of the sea and were still wet with brine.

If Syra can be identified with Homer's *Surie*, then it was the home of Eumaeus, the swineherd of Odysseus, whence he had been kidnapped as a child by his Phoenician nurse. Homer says: 'In that isle are two cities, and all the land is divided between them . . .'. [6] It might indeed be a description of modern Syra, as it confronts the traveller sailing into the harbour; for there, each on its hill dominated by a cathedral, are the twin cities that make up the capital of the island— to the right, or north, on the Vrontado hill, but covering also most of the foreshore, is the modern and Orthodox Greek Hermopolis; to the left, the old Latin town of Ano-Syra, or Upper Syra, dating back to the time of the Duchy—where we were happy to glimpse in the moonlight a tower that looked as if it might be a relic of the Venetian defences.

We found an hotel, and were recommended to the restaurant Stavropolos on the Platea Miaoulis, which turned out to be about the best restaurant we ever found in provincial Greece. It was very small and, whenever we were there, almost deserted, but it certainly knew how to cook and serve an appetizing meal, and few are the restaurants in the Greek provinces of which I would say the same.

The Platea Miaoulis is an unlikely place to find in the Aegean. It is a large rectangle, paved with marble, and dotted with palm trees, flower-beds, a band-pavilion and a statue of Admiral Miaoulis: the long side on the west is occupied by a rather grand town hall, with wings flanking a pillared portico, reached by a broad flight of marble steps; while the remaining sides of the *platea* are bounded by arcaded thoroughfares. The effect is not at all Greek. It was built in the late nineteenth century, probably under French influence, and about it is a Second Empire opulence and elegance that have unexpectedly defied the shabbiness that the tide of careless Greek life brings as inevitably as salt water brings barnacles—though it is often indeed a shabbiness that has charm. The *platea* keeps its soigné look; but it remains an exile, so much out of place that it cannot avoid a self-conscious air. Perhaps when the band plays, and a chattering crowd fills the great rectangle, it becomes properly integrated into the Greek world; or perhaps then its effect is heightened, creating the illusion of a sophisticated Riviera resort—I don't know, for we never saw it otherwise than nearly empty, when it looked coldly handsome, and very aloof from the plebeian traffic of the quay. (Plate VI)

Our hotel was close to the quay, and in consequence we had a disturbed night, for Syra is even busier than Tenos; it is the Clapham Junction of the Aegean, the one place where you can catch a boat for anywhere, and boats come and go at all hours. In fact, the night vied in discomfort with a night in a haunted grange, so full was it of clanking chains and mournful hooting, not to mention the tumbril-like rumbling of cartwheels on the cobbles of the waterfront. Tournefort had much the same experience, and he wrote that the people are 'so laborious, there's no sleeping in this Island; not in the night-time, because of the universal Din made by the Handmills, each Man works at to grind his Corn; nor in the day-time, because of the Rumbling made by the Wheels for spinning Cotton'.[7]

In the morning we set off for Upper Syra, which, like the citadel at Naxos, is still occupied by Catholics, who derive in some cases from the families of the conquest. It is a long and weary climb up an interminable sequence of steps, but all the way it is fascinating. At first the steps are a broad, straight thoroughfare bordered by large, ancient houses retiringly shuttered, with projecting balconies; but soon the steps narrow and twist among little dwellings that are squeezed together, piled up, and inextricably mingled in a fantasy of planes, of doors and windows at every level, of steps going up and steps going down, of basements above and roofs below—until at last you come to a halt no longer knowing if you are in a street or someone's backyard. And the probable answer is both. There is plenty of colour, on shutters and doors, and everything has a scrubbed look without a hint of squalor.

At the top is the Frankish cathedral and the Bishop's house; we were shown over the former by a nun, who regarded us as intriguing oddities: she spoke French, but had nothing to tell us of the church, and retired to pray while we looked round. There was indeed little she could have said, for it is a disappointing building, though I was mildly entertained by the ornate decoration that included cream pillars with gilded capitals, and a pale blue roof peppered with golden stars; but even this splendour did not much enliven the gloomy interior—however, in this last particular I may have misjudged it, since while we were there the day clouded over, and there was a thunderstorm. The most rewarding memory I have of the cathedral is the view of it one gets from beyond the town on the west, when it looks as though it had been gripped and thrust skyward by a great fist of rock.

There is nothing much to be seen inland from the summit except the taller hills circling the town, but one has a good view of the large bay within which lie the three harbours of Syra, protected by the Isle of Asses—a name reminiscent of a celebrated episode in Syra's medieval history.

At the Latin conquest Syra became part of the original Duchy of Naxos, and in 1286, when the third Duke, Marco II, was ruling, it was held by his son, Guglielmo. One day a band of pirates raided the domain of the Ghisi family, lords of Tenos and Mykonos, and carried off, among much else no doubt, an ass, which they subsequently sold to Guglielmo. Antagonism between the Ghisi and the Sanudi was never wanting, and in this matter Guglielmo's offence was deliberate, for the ass had been marked with its owner's initials. Ghisi was naturally furious. He declared war, invaded Syra, and besieged Guglielmo in his castle.

However, it fell out that at this moment a fleet belonging to Charles II of Anjou, King of Sicily, was revictualling at Melos, and Charles was now, following the death of William Villehardouin, Prince of Achaia, the suzerain of the Duke of Naxos. Also on Melos was Cassandra Sanudo, a member of the ducal family, who had charm and eloquence enough to persuade the Angevin admiral that under feudal law it was his duty to go to the assistance of the Duke's son. Accordingly, he sailed for Syra, forced Ghisi to withdraw, and put an end to the War of the Ass; but it was not the end of the commotion, and finally the Venetian Bailie of Euboea was called in to arbitrate, and was able to reconcile the two dynasties.

In the late fourteenth century Syra was given with Andros to Pietro Zeno by Francesco, the first of the Crispo dukes; but it soon reverted to the Crispi, and remained with them, except for two brief intervals when it was governed by Venice, until the Duchy fell to the Turks in 1566. At the outbreak of the Greek War of Independence in 1821, the island remained neutral, but after the Turkish massacres on Psara and Chios, it accommodated thirty thousand refugees; it was these people who built the modern town of Hermopolis on the hill opposite Upper Syra. A hundred years later, after the Turco-Greek war of 1921-2, Syra again provided a haven for refugees, and three thousand children were brought up here by an American mission.[8]

Hoping to find a few bits of the old Frankish castle, we plodded up to what appeared to be a line of towers on the western end of the hill, only to find when we arrived that we had suffered from much the same delusion that afflicted Don Quixote, and that these were the shells of ancient windmills! But among the houses on the south-east side of the hill, some distance below the summit, there is part of a small bastion, pierced by a rounded arch through which runs a path, and this looks as though it had once been a gate through the city wall. That was all we could unearth in Upper Syra; but down on the waterfront, on a small hillock at the northern end, is a round tower that we were assured by several inhabitants had a Venetian origin, and I believe this may be correct.

Having crossed over to the Vrontado hill, we were coming down through the modern city when, outside the church of Ayios Nikolaos, we were accosted by a boisterous, jaunty old fellow, with a bag over his shoulder, who might have been one of those Aegean pirates returning with his booty—and if he hadn't Long John's parrot, he at least had a cat, who tailed him with fierce determination. In fact nothing was going to keep that cat out of the bag—for, as we later discovered, it contained fish.

The old man hailed us exuberantly—we were English? Ah, he knew English. 'London! Thames! Peecadeely! Eh?' My heart sank. I feared this was going to be another game of cross-talk and crooked answers, in which, as in some Kafka-like nightmare, everything is said and nothing communicated, and all that can be done at last is to keep the one international signal flying, and fix a smile. It was not as bad as that, however: his verbs were a trifle weak, but, as Humpty Dumpty said, 'They're the proudest—adjectives you can do anything with, but not verbs'. But his key nouns were good, and it was rarely that I was driven to the last ditch, and my Greek.

He was much disappointed to learn we were not a lord and lady, nor even rich; but when it came to the final humiliating confession that we had no children, I was charmed to find he was a bachelor, and in the same case. We exchanged grave nods, but whether his was in congratulation or commiseration, I couldn't be sure. Perhaps here at last was one Greek who genuinely agreed with their saying that to have no children is bad, but to have children is too bad.

He insisted on taking us over the church, to the disgust of the cat, who followed us imploring him to get a move on. All I remember of the church was a woman sticking in silver pellets to form a name on the icing of a large cake about two feet in diameter. I asked him about this, and he told me it was a kólliva, or cake that is made in commemoration of one who has died. Consisting of wheat, almonds, sugar and spices, and, until recently, pomegranate seeds, it is prepared at a few traditional intervals after the death, on the anniversaries, and on All Souls Day. It is taken to the church, where the priest eats a morsel of it, and to the cemetery that a little may be sprinkled on the grave; at the end it is distributed to anyone and everyone.

On coming back to the quayside, we saw the old blue-painted water-cart going its rounds, which reminded me of Edmond About's account of his visit to Syra. He had come to Greece expecting 'a sky without a cloud, a sea without a ripple, an unending Spring, and above all clear rivers and cool shades'. But it rained the whole way to Syra, his first port of call, where the few trees on the island were not visible from the harbour, where 'there is neither river, nor stream, nor brook to be seen, and water is sold at one sou the glass'.[9] I imagine this kind of disillusionment is yet common among tourists, who are wont to regard it as a meteorological fact of Greek lands that 'Eternal summer gilds them yet'.

Chapter Six

NAXOS

The Kidnapped Heiress

OUR boat, the *Despina* again, left at 7.50, half an hour late. We were still travelling third, and we looked into the covered deck to see if there were any room. It was crammed. The Greeks when they travel have a yearning to lie full length if it can possibly be managed, and every square inch of the floor, gangways not excluded, was covered with bodies; even on the benches a few early comers had stretched themselves out, and acquired squatters' rights, which no-one was prepared to contest. Like the dead suitors of the *Odyssey* they, too, might have been compared to 'fishes that fishermen have drawn forth in the meshes of their net from the grey sea upon the curving beach, and they all lie heaped upon the sand, longing for the waves of the sea, and the bright sun takes away their life'.[1]

Others, who had been unable to get their six feet of deck, sat, squeezed tightly together, on the hard wooden benches, with the inevitable bundle at their feet; they looked nervously elated, as though they were putting a good face on a dire affair, for, so far as a longing for the sea is concerned, the modern Greek in no way resembles Homer's fish, and it is evident even the islanders regard a sea-trip as a precarious venture.

After one look, Aileen and I retreated, and climbed the ladder to the open deck above. Here were only a few prone forms, wrapped in blankets, and all the benches were empty.

Apparently, although the sea was like a pond, the motion, or perhaps merely the disturbing idea of being at sea, had upset one or two people: they had been sick, and a Greek is sick with the nonchalance of an animal—just where he happens to be.

The night was pleasant enough, not too cold, with a fitful moon, and we chugged along peacefully; though we were not without an uneasy feeling of perilous seas, as time and again a jagged buttress of cliff, or a lonely rock, would tower up blackly, looking horribly near and menacing, with never a light to mark it.

We lay off Paros for an hour, while passengers and freight were taken to and from the ship in small boats. I noticed one Greek couple who came aboard with no less than seven suit-cases, so that all operations were halted while he shuttled frantically up and down the ship's ladder, bringing up his belongings in relays, and looking like a competitor in some freak sporting event. No-one appeared to mind waiting, and he was quite unembarrassed, for, as is natural in a poor country, the do-it-yourself attitude is everywhere allowed for and respected.

It was past midnight when we reached Naxos—the Pearl of the Aegean, the isle of Dionysus, and the capital of the Latin Duchy. (Plate X) The town, piled on its conical hill, had a fragile look when the moon lit it, as though it had been model-led out of white cardboard; while next to it, on the peninsula —which was once an island—of Palati, the three great mono-liths that make the gateway to the temple of Dionysus loomed up startlingly against the night sky, and, confronting the bric-à-brac dwellings of men, proclaimed their status emphatically as the portal of a god.

We were able to disembark directly onto the quay, where the baggage of all passengers was collected by an elderly but active little man, who had brought along a kind of home-made mailcart. It was no use protesting you would carry your own luggage, he seized it, and tossed it into the mailcart, where a wobbly mountain soon arose. He was accompanied by his boss, or perhaps it was his partner, who, without doing a hand's turn himself, directed a stream of highly critical comment at his underling, while assuring the rest of us that all would be well. The little man took no notice. He was that rarity, a Greek who was both taciturn and efficient. When at length all the baggage had been collected, he picked up the shafts of the mailcart, tugged and strained, eventually, against all probability, got under way, and toiled off, the owners falling in behind, like a funeral cortège behind a catafalque.

But it was no procession of mutes. The mountain tottered; a suitcase fell off; cries, admonitions, commands, rose on every side. The boss, with many placatory words, retrieved the casualty, but his man might have been deaf. Thinking they were probably taking us to a hotel of their own choosing, I murmured my choice in the ear of the little man. There was no perceptible reaction—but we were deposited at the right place.

We were to see a good deal more of this individual. I never found out his name, but Aileen, who was greatly taken with him, christened him Mr Dabbs, after a character in a novel that is dear to us both. Almost as remarkable as his taciturnity was his ubiquity. We met him everywhere—and always to our advantage. There was the time when we were leaving the tourist headquarters after a fruitless inquiry about boats, when a demure cough made us turn, and there was Mr Dabbs. He beckoned to us, and led us to an office in which we obtained at least some of the answers.

Were we in doubt as to buses, or searching for a building, Mr Dabbs, as likely as not, would turn up as pat to the occasion as though I had rubbed Aladdin's lamp, and he were the genie. No matter where one was, on the quay, in a restaurant, in the lower town, or up in the old Latin citadel on the hill—anywhere in Naxos, if a problem should occur, one might expect to find Mr Dabbs materializing at one's elbow, and, in the traditional manner of an apparition, beckoning without uttering a word.

We never knew what his job really was, or whom he served, or where he lived; but once I did hear him speak. The night we left Naxos, he carried our bags to the ship. I paid him a few drachmae, and he bowed his acknowledgments; and then as the gangway rattled down, I shook hands with him, and he spoke.

'Goodbye,' he said.

Our hotel was on the primitive side, but it was clean, and run by a cheerful, obliging woman—the beds, however, were about the hardest ever. In the morning we went first to Palati, where all that is left of the temple are the great portal and a few fallen blocks of marble; but from the ruins one has a good view of the town, looking as neat as a bee-skep, of the coast, which here turns back at an acute angle north-east, and, inland, of a wall of dark hills with a coping of spiky tops. A white speck in these hills marks the tiny chapel where, according to tradition, St John once took refuge.

But it is not the saint but the god who is really linked with the island; for here it was that Dionysus, arriving in a ship he had captured from pirates, came upon the weeping Ariadne who had been ungratefully abandoned by Theseus, after she had helped him to slay the Minotaur. Dionysus married her, and later set the crown of Thetis, which his bride had worn, among the stars of heaven, where it shines today as the Corona Borealis.

On the way back from Palati we visited the local tourist office, where we found a pretty, pleasant-mannered and very well-meaning young woman, who was infuriating! The trouble was that she had a 'spiel' about every place on the island, which she was able to reel off with great fluency, but that beyond this she did not know a great deal of English. Consequently, anxious to avoid inquiries that would demand answers, she launched at every opportunity into her patter; while I, on the other hand, with all the information on sites that I needed, only wanted to know the details of the bus service.

The result left us both hiding our irritation with exquisite politeness, while Aileen tactfully turned her attention to the placards on the wall.

I began by asking the time of the first bus to Chalki. The name activated her instantly.

'Ah, Chalki!' she exclaimed. 'There, you will see——' and began to recite the glories of Chalki.

I interrupted. 'The bus,' I pleaded. 'When does it leave? Also,' I added—not yet having grasped that a name brought words to her lips as infallibly as an onion brings tears to the eyes—'also the bus for Apeiranthos?'

'Ah, Apeiranthos!' she said with relish. 'At Apeiranthos you will see——', and she was in full cry round the island before I could get in another word. At last, however, our manners at breaking point, I gathered that the bus for Chalki went at 8 a.m.—a time that proved, when we missed it next morning, to be wrong. But she was a most attractive young thing, she took a lot of trouble for us, and I feel guiltily that she would have had some excuse for exclaiming, almost in the words of young Barnacle of the Circumlocution Office, 'Upon my soul you mustn't come into the place saying you don't want to know, you know!'.

Next, we walked up to the old town on top of the hill, which had been founded by Marco Sanudo, the first Duke, at the beginning of the thirteenth century. Here he built his castle, with a central keep, and twelve towers guarding the circuit of wall.

Sanudo was in many ways a brilliant man, but altogether too ambitious, and too fond of a fight. Once established in the possession of more than a score of islands, held directly by himself or by friends who owed allegiance to him, and having received the title of Duke of Naxos from the Latin Emperor at Constantinople, he looked round for means of expanding his conquest. It became clear at this point that if the Aegean was now an Italian sea, it was by no means a Venetian appanage; for Sanudo, to the chagrin of Venice, refused from the outset to regard himself as her vassal; indeed, one of his first acts was to aid the Cretan rebellion against the Republic.

This venture ended disastrously, and he failed once more in an expedition against the Greeks, who now, under a Greek emperor, Theodore Laskaris, continued from their base at Nicaea, in Asia Minor, the war against the Franks. Sanudo was defeated, and made prisoner; at which point his fantastic career took a turn worthy of a folk tale, for he so delighted Theodore by his courage and handsome presence that he was liberated, and given the Emperor's sister in marriage.

It was, no doubt, an alliance very pleasing to the Greek subjects of the Duke. He had the wisdom to treat these consistently with tolerance and understanding, to engage their goodwill, and thus to create the best possible safeguard for his new domain; but all the same it was not on the surface a conquest that looked to be very durable. The Franks were but a small minority in a potentially hostile population, and they had many enemies—the Nicaean Greeks, the Genoese, who were continually at war with Venice, the pirates of all nationalities, and, most formidable of all, the Turks. These last being represented in the early days of the Duchy by the ships of the Seljuk Emirates in Asia Minor, and later by the mighty fleets of the conquering Ottomans.

In addition to these menaces from without, the Franks were frequently at odds with one another. The island lords who owed allegiance to the Duke were not always willing to acknowledge his rights, and the question of where feudal obligations lay was a frequent cause of quarrel; in practice these obligations tended to shift according to the pressure of circumstance, but given an opportunity, each petty baron was ready and willing to act as an independent ruler.

In 1303 when Guglielmo, the chief figure in the War of the Ass, became Duke, he was exceedingly wroth at the refusal of Jacopo Barozzi, lord of Santorin, to do him homage, and he had Barozzi abducted from a ship on the high seas, and flung into a dungeon at Naxos. Barozzi, however, had been Venetian governor of Candia, and Venice at once issued an ultimatum to the Duke, who was compelled to release his captive. But the Sanudi had no intention of abandoning their claims, and Guglielmo's son, Niccolò, attacked the Barozzi again, captured their two islands of Santorin and Therasia, and dispossessed them forever. Nor were relations between the Sanudi and Ghisi ever good; Guglielmo took Amorgos from them, and Niccolò descended on Mykonos, and carried off the reigning Ghisi's wife.

Yet, for all their turbulence, their violent and high-handed ways, the Sanudi were able men, and their dynasty ruled at Naxos for a hundred and seventy-six years, from 1207 to 1383. But in 1361 the reigning Duke, Giovanni I, died, leaving an only daughter, Fiorenza, and for the first time the Duchy came under the rule of a woman.

Fiorenza had been married to one of the dalle Carceri, who owned two of the three baronies of Euboea; but she was now a most attractive widow, with one son, a child. Not only was she still young and beautiful, but as Duchess of Naxos and the owner of the Euboean baronies, she was a great heiress; consequently there were many suitors for her hand, and a vast amount of political intrigue went on round her second marriage. The first candidate was a Genoese of Chios; but Venice would tolerate no man from among her age-long enemies as Duke, and the Duchess was warned to have nothing to do with him, while the Venetian Bailie at Negroponte was told to see to it that the affair was terminated.

The next suitor was the wealthy, influential and astute Florentine financier, Nerio Acciajuoli, who was soon to become the ruler of Corinth, and would eventually make himself Duke of Athens. Fiorenza, who was perhaps a little impressionable, took a fancy to Nerio, when they met at a hunting party in Euboea; but again Venice would have none of it—the Republic was determined that only a Venetian, or a Venetian nominee, should acquire the lady's hand.

Venice was not the suzerain of the Duchy, but, as the Republic pointed out, the Duchy had been originally won by her good-will, and had been constantly protected by her fleets and her diplomacy. Venice was indeed of far too much consequence to Naxos for the Duchess to ignore her wishes, but nevertheless Fiorenza was a Sanudo, and not much inclined to be dictated to in this particular matter by a power who had no legal rights over her; while Nerio had the backing of Robert, Prince of Achaia.

In these circumstances, Venice feared trouble, and took a very high hand. She ordered her fleet to oppose any landing of Nerio in the Cyclades, and she quietly dropped a hint to her agents, of whom she had many, in the Aegean. They moved promptly; and one day in 1364 Fiorenza was kidnapped, taken aboard a Venetian galley, and conveyed to Crete. There she was bluntly offered the alternative of marrying her cousin, Niccolò Sanudo, or of remaining a prisoner.

Niccolò was a huge, good-natured, very personable fellow, a renowned warrior, who had distinguished himself fighting against the Turkish raider, Morbassan, and had been nicknamed for his exploit 'Spezzabanda' or 'Disperser of a host'. He and the susceptible Fiorenza had not met since they were children, and now they no sooner looked but they loved; so oddly enough it happened that for once the crafty, obdurate Republic unwittingly plotted a love match.

The marriage took place in Venice, and turned out a very happy one. They were a high-spirited couple, appropriate rulers, one feels, for the romantic island state; and Spezzabanda proved to be not only a good husband, but, as Duke Niccolò II, a competent ruler.

But at the end of seven years, in 1371, Fiorenza died, having borne her husband two daughters, one of whom was the Maria whose fortunes, as the Lady of Andros, we have followed. Spezzabanda continued to act as regent, until Fiorenza's son, Niccolò III dalle Carceri, came of age and took over the duke-dom. It soon became evident that the young Duke was a thoroughly bad type. He riled Venice by treacherously attempting to seize Negroponte; while his extortionate rule provoked his own people to fury. He became hated on every hand—and there was one man, Francesco Crispo, who saw in this his opportunity, and took it.

Crispo, who had married a Sanudo, the daughter of a baron of Melos who had been Fiorenza's uncle, could contend that he had through his wife a claim to the dukedom, and he determined to make a bid for it. On a day when Niccolò was out hunting on Naxos, in the valley of Melanes some four miles south-east of Naxia, Crispo had him murdered. Immediately afterwards, making only the crudest efforts to disguise his guilt, Crispo occupied the castle at Naxos, and was at once accepted by the people as their Duke. Everything, however, depended on the attitude of Venice, and the Bishop of Melos was sent to obtain her agreement to the usurpation.

Crispo was a wily and insinuating diplomat, as perhaps the co-operation of a bishop implies, and he was able to gain over even more important people—notably the Bailie of Negroponte, whom he bribed by bestowing on his son, Pietro Zeno, the island of Andros, which Crispo took from Maria Sanudo. Venice, for her part, was not troubled by any moral scruples—she very seldom was when it came to a clear-cut issue between these and her interests; and it was certainly in her interest to have Crispo in place of the undesirable Niccolò. The new Duke was a man who could be relied on to organize a strong defence against the Turks; while, in his rather delicate situation, he would be particularly dependent on Venice. Furthermore, Crispo wisely made no claim to the baronies of Euboea, which left Venice free to gather them in. So Venice agreed to recognize Francesco I, and thus was established in 1383 the second great ducal dynasty, which was to last for another hundred and eighty-three years, until the Turks took all.

There is, I think, no more fascinating place in the Aegean than the old Latin town on the hill at Naxos. Here, in the huge rooms of crumbling mansions that have coats of arms blazoned over doors, and cut in window ledges and chimney breasts, live the members of a little Catholic community, several of whom can trace their descent back to the families of the Venetian régime, to the Barozzi, the Sommaripa, the della Rocca, or the Sforza-Castri.

Most of these old Venetian towns in the islands, which were once fortified, can show their fragments of wall and bastion, but few of them give you, as Naxos does, the feeling that you are indeed entering a citadel. With some of them altogether too much has vanished, as at Exobourgo, where the houses have disappeared, or at Upper Syra, where no defences remain, and the houses toward the summit are a mere jumble; while in other towns, like Seriphos, enough has gone to make it difficult to picture the medieval lay-out. But the old town at Naxos preserves the outline, a little blurred, of a fortress. As one winds up from the quay through the lanes of the lower town to the main gate (Plate VII) on the north-west, with its double arch and covered passage, one can see both to west and east where the great wall ran—where, indeed, it still runs, although this may not be apparent at the first glance. For bastion and rampart and chemin-de-ronde have been converted into houses, or have had houses built upon them, that now are neatly whitewashed, with modern windows and balconies; yet here and there a short length of ancient masonry, crowned perhaps by a merlon or two, plainly indicates that you are really looking at the curtain of the citadel's outer enceinte. On the east, or left as you approach the gate, there is in fact one prominent relic, a fine round tower that has kept much of its medieval aspect: today it is incorporated in a house known as the Barozzi palace. (Plate VIII) Some of these houses may be nearly as old as the wall, or may even have been built originally as a part of the wall, like the houses to be seen at Kastron in Siphnos, and have merely been modernized.

We passed through the gate, which has on its stone jamb a long vertical groove that is an old standard of measurement, a survival from the time when the merchants gathered here to bargain with the people of the citadel. Beyond the gate the way into the citadel made a sharp turn to the left, and went up through the curtain, revealing above our heads a section of battlemented wall with pointed merlons. It continued on between the high walls of houses that had once belonged to the retainers and family connections of the Duke, and that bore at intervals on their façades an escutcheon. We were to see more of these armorial bearings within the houses: particularly striking was the leopard holding a crown of the Sforza-Castri, but much the most frequent, as one would expect, were the three lozenges surmounted by two crosses of the Crispi.

The lanes of the citadel are of course too narrow and steep for wheeled traffic, and they were almost empty. It was very quiet and very hot. As one stepped time and again from the gloom of an arch into blinding sunlight, the heat struck fiercely, and the walls seemed to crowd in and give one the feeling of being resisted. Nobody met us, but now and then I glimpsed a figure eyeing us from a doorway, or flitting across the lane ahead. At the back of my mind was the conviction that we were being watched; and once when we inadvertently stumbled into the back premises of a house, and were greeted by the loud barking of dogs, I half expected the ducal guard to appear! No wonder, I reflected, if watchfulness had become second nature in a community where for so many centuries it had been the sole guarantee of safety, since any hour of the day or night had been liable to bring some brutal cut-throat to plunder and murder, or, worst fate of all, to carry one as a slave into his galleys. And even today, if this were no longer a citadel threatened by a multitude of enemies, it was at any rate a fortress sheltering a community alien in its background and outlook from those who surrounded it.

But we were to find no friendlier nor more hospitable people in all our travels than the Naxiotes of the citadel; and on the surface, which was all we could observe, there was nothing to indicate any friction between them and the Greeks of the lower town, though there might be a touch of aloofness.

At the top of the hill we emerged on to a little *platea*. On one side of this is what is left of Marco I's keep, while close at hand is the small Frankish metropolitan church, making an odd contrast with its light brown masonry erupting into greyish cupolas—putting one in mind of bubbling dough! Near by, too, are the bishop's house, and, most evocative relic of them all, the ducal palace.

The keep is now only a shell in the form of a pentagon, the wall varying from about sixty feet high on the north-west to twenty feet or so on the other, shorter sides. There is an entrance at the north-east, and although we were not able to get in, I was told that there is a room at this point containing a cistern used by the town. Adjoining the keep, built on to it in fact, on the south-west, is the famous Ursuline convent and school.

The keep, the cathedral, and the Duke's palace were all locked, the *platea* was empty, and we were wondering disconsolately how to obtain the entrée, when there came a voice from heaven, and looking up, we saw a good, French-speaking angel on a balcony, who directed us to an old lady who held all the keys except those of the keep, and would show us round.

We were taken first to the palace of the Dukes, which stands at the easternmost extremity of the enceinte, and is a tall structure built for the most part against the side of the hill, but having its third storey on the summit, where there is a chapel, with a terrace adjoining it, which can be entered on the west from the *platea*. Later in its career, the building belonged in turn to the Order of St Francis of Sales, to the Jesuits, and to the Lazarists, and the insignia of the first two appear on the front.

The chapel is a basilica, with a gallery at the back, and a high barrel roof with two clerestory windows; there is a canopied pulpit, and a reredos with gilded pillars, but the main attraction is a portrait of St Louis, in a heavy gilt frame surrounded by the fleurs-de-lis of France. It is a dark canvas that shows the saint and monarch with a crown balanced on the very top of his head, holding what would appear to be a napkin: he has a melancholy, wistful air, as well he might, and it is easier to see him as the saint than as the gallant intrepid paladin of whom we hear in the memoirs of his devoted servant, Joinville.

'Never,' exclaims Joinville, 'have I seen so fair a knight! For he seemed by the head and shoulders to tower above his people, and on his head was a gilded helm, and in his hand a sword of Allemaine.' And he relates how, at the landing in Egypt, the king

'leapt into the sea, which was up to his armpits. So he went, with his shield hung to his neck, and his helmet on his head, and his lance in his hand, till he came to his people who were on the shore. When he reached the land, and looked upon the Saracens, he asked what people they were, and they told him they were Saracens; and he put his lance to his shoulder, and his shield before him, and would have run in upon the Saracens if the right worthy men who were about him would have suffered it.'

But he was not always to be held back; and afterwards we hear how, going to the rescue of his brother, Charles of Anjou, he 'rode spurring amidst his brother's men, with his sword in his fist, and dashed so far among the Turks that they burnt the crupper of his horse with Greek fire'.[2]

A door in the south side of the chapel gives on to the terrace, which looks east over a line of battlements. The view is across a fertile valley and along the flank of purple hills that are perfectly designed to lead the eye on to the remote silhouette of Mount Zea, and to enhance the dignity of this peak, the highest in the Cyclades. South and west the terrace is bounded by wings of the palace a couple of storeys high; but they were filled with the rubble of floors and ceilings that had collapsed, and we were not able to get inside, nor to reach the floors below. Our guide had nothing more to tell us, and we naturally concluded that the lower parts of the palace were choked with debris and impenetrable. Two days later, however, we made an exciting discovery.

We were exploring along the outside of the old city wall, and came to the foot of the Duke's palace, recognizable by the terrace above—and here, at ground level, was a doorway that offered a clear entry. We scrambled up to it over the end of an outer wall, and went through into a vaulted chamber, beyond which nine stone steps led to another storey. A rough wooden staircase then brought us into a fine arched corridor eighty feet long, running north and south; and opening off this corridor on the east was a once-magnificent hall.

It was about sixty feet by fifty, and was divided into three aisles by two rows of rounded arches carried on great stone piers, each aisle being barrel-vaulted, with a tall window at its east end, and at the west a doorway giving on to the corridor. It was the roof of this hall that supported the battlemented terrace next to the chapel.

We were enchanted to have discovered what was surely the great salon of the Dukes, and one that in its heyday would have been not unworthy of them; but it was now in a pathetic state of decay. The plaster had fallen from piers and roof, leaving them piebald with crumbling patches of dirty brown, or exposing areas, like fungi, of blackened, rough rubble-and-mortar masonry; while the modern, but slightly rickety wooden floor was thick with debris that might have been the poppy dust of oblivion, the very dribble from Time's hour-glass, quietly obliterating human glory and puissance.

It was a shame to see it neglected; and once again I felt exasperated that so much effort should be given to rescuing every trace of the classical monuments, and nothing at all done to preserve the remains of this brilliant medieval world. The Dukes are dust, their good swords rust, but it is not as inevitable that their other remains should moulder, and it is regrettable that they are more often than not allowed to do so.

To return to our earlier visit; we went on to the metropolitan church, a few steps away. Founded in the thirteenth century by Marco Sanudo, it is noteworthy chiefly for the gravestones with armorial bearings that lie here and there in the floor. We discovered the arms of the Barozzi, the D'Ambri, the Crispi, the Sforza-Castri and others that we could not identify; but all the dates were after the Turkish conquest.

Leaving the church, we wandered over both the upper and lower town, fascinated by the deep, winding lanes and the recurring archways, by the manner in which fragments of ancient wall, a row of merlons, or the crumbling ruin of a tower cropped up next to a modern-looking house, or was built into a garden wall. It was as though the town were emerging with reluctance from its medieval chrysalis.

We met two helpful people, one of whom was the lady whose dogs we had disturbed. She spoke both French and English, and was kindness itself, telling us much about this Latin community. We learned that in the upper town there were about thirty-five people left who could trace their descent from the old Venetian families; she herself was by birth a della Rocca, her mother had been a Barozzi, and her grandmother on her father's side a Sommaripa. Referring to her dogs, she said her husband was by profession a hunter. This, I felt, had a fine, old-world, fairy-tale ring about it, but it seemed an odd vocation to find on a Greek island, and somewhat intrigued, I asked what he hunted.

'Oh,' she replied, 'rabbits, partridges, and'— she hesitated for a word—'birds with long necks.' Wild geese, wild duck, herons? I don't know, and I was still puzzled as to how he made a living out of this, but I felt it would be hardly polite to pursue the matter.

Our second acquaintance was the Catholic priest, Father John Marengos, a delightful person, who gave up much time to satisfying our desire for information. In his company, we paid several visits, including one to the Barozzi palace, which incorporates the tower on the north of the enceinte. The tower, alas, is now a mere shell, ruinous inside and no longer occupied. (Plate VIII) All the houses had large rooms with high raftered ceilings, or sometimes with reed thatching, with immensely thick walls and big windows, and were pleasantly airy and cool in this hot weather; but in winter, even the mild winter of Naxos, it must be difficult to keep warm in them. Most were occupied by elderly people whose sons and daughters had left them to work on the mainland; and it was plain that often there was not much money to maintain the buildings. One might have expected that this dwindling community, living in straitened circumstances amid the crumbling relics of lost grandeur, divided by religion and background from its neighbours, and with hardly any young people, would have generated a melancholy atmosphere— but nothing of the kind. Without exception, they struck us as cheerful, energetic, contented folk, always ready to laugh. Their good manners and hospitable attitude were essentially Greek qualities, but there were, too, a sophistication and grace that derived perhaps from their different cultural background, if not from their aristocratic forbears; moreover, if they were proud of their past, they were in no way backward-looking. I thought it a close-knit society; one felt an intimacy, a kind of esprit de corps among them, which is, I imagine, normal in any community that tends to be isolated.

While we were talking to our two acquaintances, the lady's husband, the hunter, arrived, and having kissed the priest's hand with great respect, greeted us very affably. He had just shot a rabbit, and appeared in high spirits, which led me to wonder if a rabbit were a notable bag in Naxos, and my curiosity about the economics of his profession revived. Was he perhaps some kind of warden, or ranger, sworn to keep the king's greenwood, and arrest poachers? But I doubted if such an official would be tolerated on a Greek island, for my impression is that every Greek with a gun considers he has an inalienable right to let fly at anything. Perhaps it was an hereditary appointment, a survival from the dukedom, a sinecure, and he was the last Grand Huntsman! It was a pleasing idea, and he had that air of courtly geniality that would have become the post—but, alas, the affair remained a mystery.

Chapter Seven

NAXOS

The Mad Duke

IN 1397, Francesco I was succeeded by his eldest son, Giacomo I, who had a lapse of manners that was extremely costly; for sailing one day into Smyrna he omitted to salute the Sultan, with the result that a Turkish fleet descended upon the Duchy, ravaged Andros, Melos and Paros, and carried off so many people that parts of the Cyclades were almost depopulated. Giacomo was followed by his brother, Giovanni II, and it was he who married the famous and formidable Duchess Francesca—one of the great figures in the story of the Archipelago.

When Giovanni died, their son was still a minor, and although her brothers-in-law, Niccolò of Syra and Guglielmo of Anaphê, were the appointed rulers, Francesca wielded much influence as her son's guardian. He had but a short reign, and his heir was a posthumous child, Gian Giacomo; so once more the Duchy came under this uneasy triumvirate of the two brothers and Francesca. But the Dowager thirsted for greater power, and finally she overplayed her hand, and demanded the regency as the child's grandmother. She made herself so objectionable that the two brothers, driven to desperation, imprisoned her. She soon regained her liberty, but her day was over. The little duke died while still in his minority; old Guglielmo of Anaphê seized the dukedom for himself; and Francesca, who had been for thirty-five years a dominating figure in the island scene, retired to Venice.

It was 1453, the year in which Constantinople fell to the Turks.

Francesca left a memorial of herself, for she had built a monastery on the shore of Naxos, and had presented it to the Knights of St John in 1452, 'in order,' says Miller, 'that she might obtain the jubilee indulgence of the *anno santo* which Pope Nicholas V had proclaimed two years before'.[1]

Of this monastery there remains only the small church of St Anthony the Hermit, near the north, or Palati, end of the harbour. We had identified it earlier, but not without some trouble, as we had mentioned it to our tourist lady, who misunderstood us, and directed us to the other end of the town! It is a plain, whitewashed basilica with the west end, fronting the sea, rising into three curves that follow the barrel-vaulting of a nave and two aisles. Within, one notices at once the delicate, almost fragile pillars that support the arches flanking the nave; some of these have been restored in a crude fashion, but time has planed the capitals of others until only faint traces remain of a leaf decoration. But on the north wall, where two arched recesses meet, a supporting pillar bears on its capital the lozenges and crosses of the Crispi. The simplicity, the austerity of ornament, the fine proportions and the worn stones combine to manifest a character that might well have been Francesca's—forthright, aristocratic, enduring, but uncompromising.

Forty-one years after Francesca's departure, Duke Giovanni III died, and as he left only illegitimate children, who were minors, Venice took over the Duchy. She found it rather more bother than it was worth: the fortifications of Naxos and the other islands needed repair; the pirates, among whom 'Paolo de Campo of Catania, half-corsair, half-hermit, and his rival, Black Hassan by name, did much damage',[2] had to be dealt with; and Venice was soon engaged in another war with the Turks, which meant her keeping a constant guard over the islands. So after six years she handed the Duchy to Francesco, the illegitimate son of Giovanni.

It was an unfortunate move; for Francesco developed into a homicidal maniac.

Nine years after his accession, when he was commanding his own galley in the service of Venice, his behaviour became so violent that the Venetian authorities put him under restraint. But they released him, and he returned to Naxos, and to Taddea Loredano, his charming and intelligent wife. Shortly afterwards, on the night of 15th August 1510, he attempted to murder her. Having been particularly affectionate and attentive, he suddenly, as she was preparing for bed, drew his sword and attacked her. She managed to get away, and clad only in her nightdress, fled through the dark lanes of the citadel to the house of her aunt, Lucrezia Loredano, the Lady of Nio.

The Lady of Nio sheltered her, but two nights later, the Duke burst into the house, where he found Lucrezia and a daughter-in-law. In a frenzy he hacked at them with his sword, and demanded his wife. A slave betrayed where she was hidden under a wash-tub: the Duke cut her over the head, and as she lay on the ground, he thrust her through the stomach. She died the next day.

Later, Francesco, sitting at table with his eleven-year-old son, Giovanni, heard that the people intended to depose him, and put Giovanni in his place. Instantly, he caught up a knife, and tried to kill his son; but the palace barber grabbed his arm, and the boy saved himself by jumping from the balcony of the room. The Duke tried to escape by sea; but the people prevented him, and after a fight in which he was wounded, he was made prisoner, and deported to Santorin.

Venice was immediately informed. She confirmed the appointment of Giovanni, and reluctantly took over the administration again during his minority, appointing the murdered woman's brother, Antonio Loredano, as the first governor. A year later, Francesco died in prison at Candia.[3]

From then onward the history of the Duchy was that of swift decline into the hands of the Turks. Hardly had Giovanni begun to rule when the unlucky youth was in peril once more and was kidnapped by Turkish corsairs; Venice quickly ransomed him, but one misfortune followed another in his long reign. In 1522 the Knights were driven from Rhodes. Ten years later the Turks descended on Naxos, and Giovanni had no recourse but to buy them off. He could ill afford it, and soon the process had to be repeated on a larger scale; for in 1536–7, Barbarossa carried fire and slaughter through the islands, and Giovanni was compelled to promise an annual tribute of five thousand ducats—and even so, Naxos was pillaged.

Giovanni's son, Giacomo IV, was the last Christian ruler of the Duchy: giving up all attempt to cope with an impossible situation, he concentrated blithely on making merry while he could. Indeed, in those last days a fever of gaiety spread through all the doomed baronies, and the Latin régime passed away to the sound of music and revelry in the citadels. Nor was the gaiety always innocent; and the Greeks of Naxos, scandalized by the debauchery of their rulers, finally, in 1566, complained to the Sultan. That was the end. Giacomo hastened to Constantinople with a bribe; but it was too late. He was deposed, and imprisoned; and although later he was freed, and fought against the Turks at Lepanto, the Duchy went to the Sultan's Jewish favourite—who bore what is to our ears the ironical name of Joseph Nasi. Eventually, the Duchy was annexed to the Turkish empire. Only Tenos, in Venetian hands, remained to the Latins until, later on, the Gozzadini, miraculously, returned to Siphnos and some other islands, where they lingered until 1617.

The next morning, having followed our tourist lady's instructions, and missed the 7.30 bus, we caught another bus at eleven o'clock to Apeiranthos. This is a hill town that lies some fifteen miles or so by road from Naxia, beyond the central ridge of mountains running from north to south down the island.

The bus, with only a few people in it, was waiting on the quay when we arrived. Hardly had we taken our seats, when there was a slight bump, and a woman in the seat in front stood up with a piercing scream. It was followed by an uproar, as everyone in and around the bus joined in happily to vociferate their alarm or indignation or merely their eager interest. It appeared that a man leading a donkey and cart had cut his corner too fine, and a wheel had struck the open door of the bus. It was trivial. There was no damage done. But all made the most of this blessed opportunity to break the tedium of the daily round. The accusations, the impassioned defence, the dramatic interpolations of lookers-on, the whole emotional release was enjoyed to the full; and when it was over, and the last declamation had died away, the woman in front turned to give us a complacent smile, aware that she had seized her cue with commendable promptitude, and launched the affair in style.

The road to Apeiranthos lies through a great fertile cup in the hills formed by the valleys of Trayiá and Drymalia; in a few minutes one is quite removed from the scorched earth and naked rock, the lean, brown, bony frame of the normal Greek island. For here are green shade, and running water and trees—planes, oaks, chinars, olive and lemon groves—scented thyme, exotic shrubs with scarlet berries, and among the trees patches of root crops. In fact a sample of the poet's Arcadia, which, in spite of the map, is so hard to light upon in Greece. Dotted through it are several fortified houses that date back to Venetian times, and there is a notably fine tower in Chalki; but we had no time to examine it. Our bus passed through Chalki and Filoti, and began to wind up rocky foothills, and we became abruptly aware of the barrier of hills surrounding this happy valley; particularly towards the north, they were a rough lot, toothed and beaked and standing over three thousand feet at Zea. From the head of the pass, north of Zea, we were able to look down into the next fertile plain, and see Apeiranthos perched on a small eminence.

It is a town that has a legendary reputation as a nest of robbers and outlaws—a town founded by Barabbas, say the other Naxiotes! There appears to have been some ground for the charge of lawlessness; at any rate when Bent visited it in the late nineteenth century, the mayor admitted to him that: 'There are some bad people among us, who live by piracy, though of late years their number has been greatly reduced'! And Bent confessed to some trepidation when the inhabitants, clad in long hairy coats, for it was cold, gathered about him like 'conspirators in a chorus'. He noticed particularly 'their large noses, which they screwed up when they laughed, and which increased their sinister appearance'.[4] It is perhaps not unreasonable that long noses, which were associated with military skill in Wellington and his officers, should also indicate piratical efficiency!

We saw no sinister noses, nor anything else to alarm us, but it was apparent that if Apeiranthos had given up its predatory habits, it held on tenaciously to its ancient ways in other matters. The old national costume was still being worn by many of the men; we found women doing their spinning in the street, and for once we encountered a reluctance to be photographed.

The national dress of the men is reminiscent of both the Turk and the corsair: very baggy dark blue breeches, with stockings and shoes, a sleeveless coat over a white shirt, a scarlet cummerbund, and a white turban, or sometimes a red beret-like cap with a black tassel. We saw no woman in costume at Apeiranthos, but later, on Kythnos, where our visit coincided with that of the King and Queen of Greece, we watched both men and women dancing in their national dress. The dress varies of course from island to island, but on Kythnos the women wore a black skirt to their ankles, a white apron and blouse, with the single exotic touch of a long mantilla, or lace scarf, that went over the head, round the neck, and fell, one end behind and one in front, almost to their knees. In spite of the scarf, it was a rather dowdy rig-out, reminiscent of a Victorian housemaid wrapping up against the draught!

The Kythnos men wore sober black coats and breeches, but their sash of scarlet and gold was colourful enough; they, however, were young men who had only put on the dress to dance before the Royal couple, and they wore it with a discernibly sheepish air—whereas here in Apeiranthos it was the old men who clung to the dress, and, carrying it with the nonchalance of habit, they looked really distinguished.

We went first to the tower that is all that remains of the castle at Apeiranthos: square, of three storeys, it is built on an outcrop of rock, and underpinned on the south by a large arch. The entrance, on the west, at the level of the second storey, is surmounted by the leopard and crown of the ubiquitous Sforza-Castri, while an inner door has the date 1677 on its lintel. The tower has had a good deal of modern cobbling, and although the outer walls with some of the arches of the windows remain, there is nothing of much interest here, except the view. Nor did that detain us long; for the fact is that the second storey was being used as a pigsty, and the upper one as an unofficial public latrine, so it was no place to linger in! As for the lower storey, we could not find any means of getting into it, and were content to leave it, an unexplored Bluebeard's chamber.

If they treat their castles somewhat rudely, the people of Apeiranthos keep the rest of their town respectable enough. It is clean, though not exactly neat; for this ancient pirate lair is a jumble of dark buildings with a guarded and secretive look. No doubt whatever it was built as a fortress and a refuge: the streets twist through what were once bastions, narrow lanes burrow through arches that are veritable tunnels, and disappear in the gloom like subterranean escape routes. Now and again a colourful, medieval figure lounges through the dark alleys—and one is overtaken by the hallucination of being back in the notorious heyday of the town. (Plate IX)

In fact Apeiranthos plays up splendidly to its reputation; and, incidentally, it put on an attractive performance for us in our lunch hour. For we sat outside a small restaurant at a table on a terrace at the top of a long flight of steps leading up from the tiny *platea*. Opposite was a *kapheneîon* with tables outside it, and near by was a plane tree, but the *platea* was in reality no more than a narrow street, which the steps, affording seats, and the cafés, had brought into use as a convenient meeting-place. From where we sat it looked like a stage set viewed from the dress circle, with a backcloth narrowing the stage, and exits right and left; and here the characters of the village comported themselves before us like a well-drilled chorus—men sitting at the table and drinking, women hurrying rather timidly across, a mule and its driver plodding on and off, or occasionally a child darting by. They were building up an entrance, and it came. A magnificent figure in wide blue breeches, in sash and tunic and scarlet cap, a corsair to the life, strode on stage. I half expected he would turn towards us, burst into a rich tenor, and declaim his love or his valour; and when, after a haughty glance round, he made a dignified exit, we both itched to give him a clap.

I thought I would like his photograph, and finding an Americano among the men below, I asked him if there would be any objection to this. To my surprise, he said there certainly would, and I must on no account do so. These men did not 'think it good' to be photographed.

This of course is the feeling among Moslems, but the people of Apeiranthos are of Cretan descent, and I have never heard of any colony of Turks or other Moslems among them, so I can only imagine they borrowed the prejudice against the making of images from their conquerors. It was not, however, by any means an attitude shared by all those who wore the costume, for later in the day we found ourselves chatting to one of them, and Aileen daringly ventured to ask if he would be photographed. He was enchanted. Certainly he would be photographed—and with the lady, if she would consent, whereupon he slipped his arm through hers, and exuberantly drew her close to him while Aileen smiled wanly at the camera, obviously feeling that her Turk had turned out a Tartar!

After returning to Naxia, we rashly visited our tourist lady again, with a view to finding out if it were possible to get from Naxos to Santorin in the next day or so. She told us that the Elli would be sailing on the following day, Tuesday; but in the morning the Elli agent told us the boat had been withdrawn for the season. He thought the Limnos might be sailing on Thursday. We hurried to the Limnos agent. He was out. We found the Despina agent, who was also of the opinion that the Limnos would be sailing on Thursday, but he added that he thought she would visit many small islands and that, starting at 10 p.m., she would not reach Santorin until 2 p.m. the following day. It was, we decided, an occasion for extravagance —we would travel first-class, and book a cabin. But the Limnos agent was still missing; no one seemed quite certain that the ship would come, and finally, becoming tired and sceptical, we gave it up for the moment. The way of a ship in the Aegean is, indeed, not easily to be known.

We caught a bus to Chalki, the conductor of which was a highly intelligent and efficient child, who looked about ten years old. From Chalki we walked to the Apanocastro, or Upper Castle, which had been built in the latter part of the thirteenth century by the third Sanudo duke, Marco II. The story runs that there had been in this part of the island an altar to a certain Saint Pachys, or Saint Fat, who was supposed by the people to have the power of rendering children plump; and in order to invoke his aid, mothers brought their skinny offspring, and passed them through a perforated stone attached to the altar. Marco, however, disapproved, and destroyed the altar. He seems to have been normally a sensible man, and it would be interesting to know what moved him, whether his Christian spirit revolted at an obviously pagan custom, or whether he were just intolerant of superstition. At any rate he did away with the altar, and it turned out a most expensive demolition; for it provoked great unrest, and he was forced to build the Apanocastro to overawe his subjects.

The castle lies on a steep hill about an hour's walk from

Chalki in a north-westerly direction. After passing the village of Tsikalarió, we followed a path that wound over a ridge and through hills of a startling and macabre appearance. Of pale grey rock, and littered with monstrous boulders, they were quite barren except for low, withered pads of prickly sage, and presented a burnt-out, end-of-the-world look. The castle was on such a hill, and merged so perfectly with the grey rock that it was difficult to pick out.

It was far gone in ruin. We had approached it from the south, where there had been a large outer enceinte, but of this there remained only a circular tower at the south-east, part of a square tower farther west, and two buildings that looked as if they had been recently rebuilt as chapels. The circular tower was the main attraction, having two storeys above the ground floor, each provided with a wall-walk carried on the arches of embrasures; the parapet at the top was gone, but it was at least a recognizable defence work, in better condition than anything else there.

It was quite a scramble up to the wall of the inner enceinte, which ran, a few feet high on the outside, round the oval top of the hill. We toiled up past the square tower, dislodging stones that fell with a staccato rattle in the absolute stillness. On the summit, at the west end, were the remains of a hall, or chapel, and of a tower abutting on it; but the keep, which had probably stood about fifty yards east at the highest point of the hill, had vanished.

Nothing could be identified with any certainty, except the course of the wall bounding the inner enceinte. Yet these fragments of masonry engendered an atmosphere, and one that, oddly enough, tended to lift the spirits. They were a relic of intelligent design in this chaotic desolation, a reminder of humanity's existence that was cheering in a world where a few melancholy birds, black and grey like half-caste crows, were the only living things.

We walked back the eight or nine miles to Naxia through the three riverside villages of Potamia, of which Middle, or Mesopotamia, is perhaps the prettiest. On the way we came across the agave in bloom. The Greeks call it *athánatos*, or 'immortal', for it was once believed to live for a hundred years before flowering; it does take a long time—then, like an anti-aircraft gun emerging from camouflage, the barrel of the great flower axis shoots up twenty feet or more. It puts out little branches of flowers, and from a distance looks rather like a young Scotch fir.

On Wednesday morning the *Limnos* agent was still absent, and we could get no confirmation of whether the ship would come. We spent the day revisiting the citadel, and in the evening walked out to the chapel of St John, on the hill behind the town: a tiny place, with a built-up façade behind which the body of the chapel is cut out of the rock. From it one has a good view to the east coast of Paros, where lies Drio Bay to which the Turkish Capitan Pasha brought his fleet every year to collect the tribute money from the islands.

The islands came off fairly well under the Turks, for owing to the perils of the Aegean, due to the galleys of the Knights, the pirates, and the potential menace of a Venetian fleet, the Turkish hold was never so firm here as on the mainland. Indeed, towards the end of the eighteenth century there were islands whose only contact with the Turks was this yearly visit of the Capitan Pasha.

Naxos, however, suffered much internal discord; for the Latins and the Greeks, so far from uniting against the common enemy, remained bitterly at odds. 'The Grand Signor,' wrote Tournefort, 'never need to fear any Rebellion in this Island: the moment a Latin stirs, the Greeks give notice to the Cadi; and if a Greek opens his mouth, the Cadi knows what he meant to say before he has shut it.' [5]

But there was not only this antagonism between the races, there were grim hereditary vendettas among the Latins themselves. At the end of the seventeenth century, for example, Ferdinand Barozzi, the leader of the Latins, murdered a certain Constantine Cocco, who had insulted Barozzi's wife. There were reprisals in kind; and at one point the Barozzi family even persuaded a visiting galley of the Knights to turn its guns on the monastery of Ipsile, where the Cocco family had taken refuge. The feud was finally ended by a Romeo and Juliet marriage between the daughter of the murdered Cocco and the son of her father's murderer. But here, too, the marriage was not the end of the story; for after the couple had spent many happy years together, the Turks began to look askance at the wealth of the husband—they threw him into prison; and he died a beggar.[6] It is a narrative whose implications convey a pretty good idea of conditions under the Turkish régime.

During the First World War, the Cyclades were occupied by the British. On Naxos, as Sir Compton Mackenzie notes in his reminiscences, there was a little trouble with the men of Apeiranthos. They declared: 'There is no reason why we should be ruled by anybody except ourselves'; and they repelled an attack by Venizelist troops.[7] In the Second World War Naxos was in the possession of the Italians, and later of the Germans, who, in October 1944, were attacked by a force made up of two British motor launches, a British liaison officer and wireless signaller, and twenty-four men of the Greek Sacred Company. Richard Capell, who was present as a war correspondent, has related what happened. The allies began by capturing the German commander, who mistook the launches for German boats, and on finding out his mistake too late, dissolved into tears. After a parley had come to nothing, the launches opened fire with their two-pounders on the citadel, in support of a land attack by the raiders and the local Andartes. The main objective was the Ursuline convent, which had been fortified, and mounted a mortar on its roof. Little impression was made by the bombardment; but at the end of the second day, a third launch joined the attackers, bringing twenty-four more men of the Sacred Company under Colonel Kalinski. Then, on the third day, the Beaufighters arrived.

'They came streaking down [writes Capell], there were crashes, and it was like an avenging deity. Within minutes the big buildings were irretrievably ablaze. The motor-launches contributed all they had, and amid what we saw were Kalinski's mortar explosions. The raiders' assault followed. But the garrison, driven to shelter in the dungeons of their citadel, had had enough. There was, we were to hear, something of a scrap with Kalinski's men in the corridors; and then surrender.' [8]

Fortunately, the damage was more or less confined to the convent, which had subsequently to be rebuilt.

At last, on Thursday, we found the agent of the *Limnos* back in his office, and, to our relief, he confirmed that the boat was due to arrive at 10 p.m. We duly booked a first-class cabin, not without a guilty feeling on my part that this betokened some slackening of the moral fibre!

At ten o'clock we marched down to the harbour behind Mr Dabbs, who had our luggage on his mailcart. With us was a middle-aged Englishwoman, who had appeared suddenly at our hotel, and who was happily jaunting alone round the isles, and was now off to Amorgos, which she had 'a fancy to see'. She was a widow, and every two years, which was as often as she could manage, she fled from England to Greece, in spite of the protests of her family, who evidently thought that a lone female in Greece was running fearful risks. Or perhaps they were of those who feel that it is as unbecoming to be a solitary traveller as a solitary drinker, and that, over the water as over the wine, company is the only excuse for indulging.

The boat of course was late, and Mr Dabbs mutely set chairs for us outside a little café near the quay. It was another of those long waits, of which we have known many—on hard chairs in the soft Greek night, listening to water lapping and the murmured gabble of voices, and feeling a mounting expectation as the moon turns on her melodramatic limelight, the stars tremble with anticipation, and all the world is alert for that long harsh challenge, which comes out of the darkness as defiantly as the note of Childe Roland's horn.

We sat there, hardly speaking. Nothing seemed to be moving except a number of large, red, beetle-like insects, which dropped around us, and, apparently unable to take off again, began to crawl frantically about the pavement.

At eleven o'clock the ship arrived.

We went down to her.

Mr Dabbs uttered his word, and melted into the crowd; his partner's voice rang out in reproof; the baggage of new arrivals piled up in the mailcart. . . . It was rather depressing to watch this life cycle beginning again.

Chapter Eight

SANTORIN

The Dowry that Reverted

As we waited at the ship's office to obtain cabins, the Englishwoman was in front of us. The chief steward explained to her in halting English that the boat would call at two ports in Amorgos, at Aiyáli and Katápoula—which did she want? It was plain she had heard of neither, but she made up her mind at once.

'Oh,' she said brightly, 'I'll take Aiyáli, it sounds nice.'

This, I thought enviously, was the ideal attitude. Planning is definitely inimical to enjoyment in these waters, and so far as the locals are concerned, it simply isn't done. Perhaps they feel, too, and no doubt rightly, that to plot one's course, to forecast one's tomorrow, is to infringe on the prerogative of the gods, and to fall into hubris. I wished we could abandon ourselves just to 'messing about in boats', taking them as they come, for it is, after all, the voyaging that is the supreme delight of Aegean travel.

It was a conclusion that I had occasion hurriedly to revise a few minutes later when we were shown to our cabin. It was a very hot night, and the cabin was stifling. The porthole, according to a steward, could not, or must not, be opened, and the air-conditioning, as he admitted with a gay smile, was not functioning. We debated whether we should sit up in the lounge, but finally decided, with an illogical but obstinate reluctance to cut our losses, that we would make an effort to get our money's worth! Perhaps when the ship began to move a draught might somehow penetrate to us; so we propped open the cabin door, undressed, and lay melting and miserable.

However, both of us went to sleep; and then, in the small hours while it was still dark, we were awakened by a thunderous knocking on the open door.

'Aiyáli!' cried a voice excitedly.

I opened one eye, and mumbled that we were going to Santorin.

The voice refused to accept this.

'Aiyáli!' it cried again, with a note of pleading.

I opened both eyes, and repeated firmly, like a countersign: 'Santorin!'

The voice muttered plaintively, and died away.

I hoped it would find the Englishwoman in time; though it hardly seemed to matter if her fancy for Aiyáli turned out to be a passing fancy, since there were so many other fascinating names from which to choose. I felt a little sad that I was not getting off at Aiyáli—it did sound attractive. Perhaps, I went on thinking sleepily, perhaps we ought to have accepted the voice as that of Fate summoning us to an unplanned adventure. But I am afraid

> 'This is the tale of the man
> Who heard a word in the night',

and went to sleep again!

We awoke once more in the dark; but the cabin was as hot as ever, so we dressed, and went up on deck. It was shortly after five o'clock, and we found the boat at rest in the bay of Katápoula at Amorgos. Presently, in the cold light before sunrise, we could see the little town looking as though it were being hustled into the sea by a bunch of stalwart, black-browed hills. The boats were shuttling to and fro, but there was no sign of our compatriot, and we concluded she had heard the voice in time.

It was nearly an hour before the Limnos got under way again and began to steam south to Anaphê. The lonely rock of

Anedro showed up almost directly on our course, while away to port we could see the pale shadow of Astypalaia; shortly before nine we were hove-to off Anaphê. I looked at the island with interest, since this was the heritage of old Guglielmo, who had had the temerity to imprison the Duchess Francesca, and who had eventually become Duke himself. Anaphê passed to his daughter, who was still ruling here at the end of the fifteenth century; later it came into possession of the Pisani, but soon afterwards it fell to Barbarossa in the great raid of 1536, and remained Turkish until the War of Independence.

Anaphê is a remote and desolate island, and one could well believe that Guglielmo's desire to leave it was among the reasons that prompted his strenuous efforts to acquire the Duchy. The coast on this southern side was high and steep-to, and there was no real harbour, only a depression in the hills that debouched on the sea by a narrow break in the cliffs. Here were two or three buildings behind which a path wound up the cliff on the left to the Chora, where are the ruins of Guglielmo's castle.

It was Anaphê that gave refuge to the Argonauts on their return from Colchis, and a temple to Apollo Aeglites was set up on the island in commemoration of the Argo legend.

Some remains of the temple are to be seen at the eastern end of Anaphê, where an isthmus connects the island to the great rock of Mount Kalamos. Kalamos is a block of marble that rises almost sheer to over a thousand feet, to a three-pronged, razor-edged crest, where there is a chapel of the Virgin. The temple ruins, with the monastery of Kalamiotissa built on the site, are lower down on the isthmus, while farther west are the remains of the ancient capital.

We had a fine view of Kalamos from the boat, and longed to do the walk up on the ridge, from the monastery to the chapel, which had given Scott O'Connor a thrill. 'On attaining the ridge,' he writes, 'upon which the chapel of the Virgin stands like an oblation up to heaven, we stand upon a blade-edge, no more than a yard in width, and the sheer fall of the cliffs upon either side to the sea is alarming.'[1] It was, however, impossible for us to find time to stay on Anaphê, and we could only look, and sigh.

Two or three small boats came out to us, one of them towing a live bullock at the end of a rope attached to its horns. As soon as the boat had reached the ship, the rope was looped over the hook of a derrick, and the animal was drawn up from the water, over the rail, and dumped aboard. It looked a shockingly brutal method, but the victim did not appear to mind: he remained perfectly quiet during the transit, and as soon as his hooves touched the deck, he stood up without any hint of discomfort.

By eleven o'clock we were steaming into the far-famed bay of Santorin, which is in fact the crater of a living volcano that has erupted at intervals down the ages, and as lately as 1956. The huge harbour is formed by the crescent of Santorin on the east and north, and the islands of Therasia and Aspronisi on the west, while in the centre are the three islands, of cinders and lava, thrown up at various periods by the volcano. They are truly named the Kaimeni, or Burnt Islands, and whether it were a fact, or simply the wind blowing the pumice dust, they seemed to be smoking. As we came by them, Aileen remarked that the water was like mother-of-pearl, with an odd milky iridescence; it has the property of cleaning the hull of a ship from barnacles and weeds, so that caiques can be given a trouble-free careening by mooring them off the Kaimeni for a night or two.

It was a fantastic scene, for opposite these islands that had risen from the Pit, and might well have been blasted by the everlasting fire, were the pumice cliffs of Santorin, unearthly and unbelievable in their garish colours—green, yellow, chocolate, purple, and to the north at Oia, a sultry red. Along the crest of them, nine hundred feet up, ran a thin white line of houses, and the effect was that of a rich, iced, Brobdingnagian cake. So flamboyant, so unlikely was it, that one might have sailed into the chimerical land of a traveller's tale: beautiful but oddly disconcerting, it left one faintly tense; one could fancy that somewhere in this bizarre world slept the ogre who had bitten into that mighty cake. Nor was it a wild fantasy. He is there, and every time he wakes, he devours a few of the inhabitants.

The harbour was once thought to be bottomless, and when, about the year 1413, Duke Giacomo I tried to sound it, he failed. Actually, it is over a thousand feet deep, and ships cannot anchor there; nor can steamers come into the quay, as a ledge of rock juts out here not far beneath the surface.

There are a few buildings at the quay, but the traveller needing accommodation must climb the eight hundred steps of the great zigzag up the cliff to the town of Thera on top. If he is wise he will go on a mule; we decided to send our baggage on a mule, and walk up, taking our time—it was a mistake, for these steps, however slowly you go, are heartbreaking. The locals, sitting on the parapet of the stairway, watched us sardonically as we laboured up, no doubt reflecting on the meanness of the rich tourist who would go to this length to save a few drachmae! I entirely agreed—we hadn't realized what a grind it would be. But Aileen raised a laugh among them by panting resignedly 'Pollé skála!', which was the nearest she could get to 'This is one hell of a staircase!'. They quite understood.

At the top, the effect is startling, for one appears to be practically overhanging the tiny port, while the cliffs beneath have a scree-like, unstable look, as though at any moment they might crumble into the sea. Nor is this by any means an unknown occurrence, for later, at Skaros, we were to see the result of it.

We found rooms in a large hotel that was nearly empty. The proprietor, who was very much of a character, with an ebullient sense of humour, spoke English with little knowledge but with immense élan, thrusting ahead with abandon, leaping from foothold to foothold over crevasses where syntax had totally disappeared, and leaving one diverted if not always wiser. He had dramatic stories to tell of the earthquake in 1956, when his hotel became a refuge for many inhabitants whose homes were crashing. Raising his clenched fists, shaking them fiercely, and growling deep in his chest, he created a vivid impression of the unnerving accompaniments of a 'quake.

He pointed out the way to Skaros, the site of the most famous of the Venetian castles on the island; and in the afternoon we made our way to it. It is a promontory about a mile or so to the north, and one reaches it by walking along the crest of the cliff, through straggling Thera, and the next village of Merovigli—whose name, according to one theory, derives from Graeco-Latin 'hemero-vigilia', meaning the place where the day-watch was posted, to give warning of an approaching enemy. It has suffered badly from earthquakes, and though a certain amount of rebuilding could be seen, the slope of the hill fronting Skaros was covered with wreckage.

Skaros is about seven hundred feet high, a steep pyramid of red pumice, crowned by a flat-topped, rocky stump like a decayed molar; it is joined to the higher cliffs of Merovigli by an isthmus at a much lower level, and to reach this one has to clamber down a dusty, skiddery track on the cliff face.

The castle at Skaros was built by the Barozzi to whom Santorin fell at the Conquest; but they lived most of the time on their estates in Crete. They never got on well with their overlords, the Sanudi: there was the incident, already referred to, at the beginning of the fourteenth century, when Jacopo Barozzi was kidnapped by order of the reigning Duke; and some thirty years after this, Niccolò I took Santorin from them. It remained with the Sanudi until 1383, when it went with the whole Duchy to the usurper, Francesco Crispo.

Duke Giacomo III, great-grandson of Francesco, and grandson of that Niccolò who, with Guglielmo his brother, had imprisoned the Duchess Francesca, gave away Santorin as his daughter's dowry on the occasion of her marriage to Domenico Pisani in 1480. It was a time of great rejoicing throughout the Duchy, following the conclusion of a peace between Venice and Turkey, and the wedding was attended with unprecedented festivities. Giacomo, who, not without some reason, was greatly charmed by his son-in-law, inducted the young couple into their island at an impressive ceremony held at Skaros. Pisani received first the keys of the castle, and then the homage of the great families of the island, including the tenacious Gozzadini, who held the castle of Akrotiri; the Pisani flag was broken out, and the bells were rung. The new ruler took measures at once to add to the prosperity of his new domain, and it looked as though a brighter era was at hand for what had been a rather neglected island.

But, unfortunately, the bride had a wicked uncle; and when, this same year, Giacomo died, the uncle succeeded him as Giovanni III. Giovanni was furious at Santorin being alienated from the Crispi, and he took violent action. He landed on the island while Pisani was absent, occupied Skaros, drove off the Venetian force that came to aid Pisani, and continued to hold the castle while the matter was brought to judgment at Venice. Pisani was the son of the Duke of Candia, and could presumably exert a good deal of influence, but Giovanni eventually won, and was allowed to keep Santorin on payment of compensation to Pisani.

The island went to the Turks with the rest of the Duchy in 1566; but after that there was the extraordinary interlude of the Gozzadini, who held on to the castle of Akrotiri, and to the islands of Siphnos, Kythnos, Kimolos, Polionos, Pholegandros, Gyaros and Sikinos, until the year 1617.

When Tournefort visited Skaros at the outset of the eighteenth century, he found there a small town in which most of the gentry lived. In addition to the castle, there were the residences of the Greek bishop, the Latin bishop, the French consul, and a house of the Jesuits—in fact it must have been 'a goodly heape for to behould'. But today it is very difficult to conceive that so much existed here, for practically everything has fallen into the sea, and the rock itself is decaying into red ruin.

The isthmus, which is of course the only approach, is at the north-east; it is quite narrow, and about a hundred and fifty yards long; at one time there was a causeway erected on it with, presumably, a drawbridge, but nothing remains of it now but a jumble of fragmented masonry, and the relics of three sunken vaulted rooms. As we walked across this neck of land, the stump of rock towered above us, an empty pedestal upon which the castle proper with its keep had once stood; while the outer enceinte had encircled the cliff at some distance below the stump, where we could still see traces of walls and bastions. But on the stump itself there was no sign of fortifications, until we reached the south-west side, where, high up, was a rude embrasure, and a stretch of wall. A trifle nervously, we decided to try and climb up by the embrasure to the top of the stump, and after a little trouble we managed it. But the only interesting object on top was an underground vaulted cistern at the south-west end, though stones and debris from the ancient works had been piled up tidily into a low wall.

It could never have been a very strong castle, not at least in the days of artillery, because the hill of Merovigli commands it. But it is an exhilarating viewpoint, and incidentally in spring it must be brilliant with flowers, for there were clumps of the wild chrysanthemum, which the Greeks call mandilída, and which makes a fine splash of yellow, and Aileen noted bugloss, saltwort, white horehound, Jerusalem sage, tree tobacco, and several fair-sized bushes of orache—now, however, only thyme was in bloom, with a few pink and white flowers on the bugloss. Either way the view was enchanting: across the harbour to Therasia; or, toward Thera, along the line of those exotic ramparts poised over water of a spellbound tranquillity, their colours washed in gold now by a level sun, looking so completely fabulous that they might have been, as one theory holds they are, a fragment of lost Atlantis—or the shore of that land mentioned by Herodotus where the one-eyed Arimaspians steal the gold of the griffins!

The next day we hired a taxi, and, accompanied by our hotel proprietor, drove to the castle of Akrotiri, or La Ponta, as it was known to the Latins, which occupies a hill, not far from the sea, at a point where the southern horn of the Santorin crescent curves round to the west. On the way to it, we paid a visit to the little marble chapel of St Nicholas, known as the Marmarina, which is actually a Greek temple of the third century B.C. It is tiny, but immensely dignified—although one is inclined to fancy that it carries its cross with a slightly awkward air!

There is a general idea that the Gozzadini were able to hold on to Akrotiri because of the strength of the castle; but this is certainly not the case. They managed to stay by keeping on good terms with the Turks; for Akrotiri, like Skaros, was by no means a formidable stronghold. The hill on which it stands rises gently, it is in fact a mere bump, and the defences were nothing out of the ordinary. It, too, has been badly knocked about by earthquakes, and is in very poor shape. The main gate, on the west, with its flanking towers, lies at the end of a lane turning off a street in the village; it is a rectangular, unimposing entrance giving on to a passage, vaulted at first, that ascends sharply to the keep. This is a square building that has been used until fairly recently as living quarters; its roof has been reconstructed, its battlements have gone, and it looks like a late nineteenth-century urban mansion in shocking disrepair! Beyond it, going east, one comes to a large vaulted chapel, and then to an arched gate leading to the outer enceinte with remains of a curtain and bastions.

It is hard to get up much enthusiasm for this sprawl of debris, of shattered barrel-vaulted rooms gaping at the sky, for the bourgeois, down-at-heel keep, the rather squalid main gate, and the rabble of masonry that straggles enigmatically over the hill. No doubt the effect is mainly due to earthquake, which, unlike time, lends no dignity where it destroys, but seems to add degradation to ruin.

It was near Akrotiri that, in the early part of 1967, a team of

Greek and American archaeologists under the direction of Professor Marinatos discovered a Minoan city buried like Pompeii under volcanic ash and pumice.

From Akrotiri the car took us down to the east coast near the little town of Kamari, where there were a few houses on the sea shore. In one of these lived a friend of our Greek companion—a man, he explained, who after some domestic trouble had given up his home in Athens, and come to this remote spot to follow the life of a recluse. A little man, whose face, with its prominent nose and chin, reminded me of portraits of Henry of Navarre, he was, I thought, an abnormally gregarious recluse. He kept up a continual banter with our friend, produced karpoúzia and frankósukia—red-fleshed water melons, and the fruit of the prickly pear—for us to eat, and finally brought out a guitar, sent to him by his son in America, and began to play to us. On the whole it looked as though he had found his métier, that solitude had for once lived up to the sages' opinion of her, and had seduced her man without leaving him melancholy.

We drove next up the newly made, zigzag motor road that climbs Mesavuna, the ridge on which are the ruins of the ancient city of Thera—most beautiful of Greek sites. The long street, bordered with the remains of temples and shops and houses, of a stoa and a theatre, runs along a rocky terrace more than a thousand feet above the sea, and offers intoxicating views of limitless sea and sky, of mountains at hand, of Anaphê a stone's throw away, of islands mingling with the clouds on the horizon. To walk here for a short while between heaven and earth, to live and move and have one's being amid such beauty, is to walk indeed in the Greek world, in Elysium.

But lovely as the site is, it has its drawback when the meltémi blows. It is so windy that the street at one point had to be built with a traverse to afford shelter, and avoid offering a funnel for the air. Baron Hiller von Gaertringen, who excavated Thera at his own expense, had to shift the work continually, as the wind veered, to get shelter; one of his mules, loaded with pottery, was blown clean off the mountain track, and 'finds' had to be brought down on sledges.

The ruins date mainly from the centuries immediately following the death of Alexander, but the city was founded in the seventh century B.C., and some of the remains, notably the temple of Apollo Karneios, go back almost to that time. It was on the dancing floor next this temple that naked youths danced at the festival in honour of the god, and inspired those messages, still to be seen, that were carved by their admirers on the adjacent rocks.

Rarely have we left a place with greater regret. It was our last expedition in Santorin; for at eight o'clock the following morning we walked down those interminable steps to board the *Despina*.

It is twenty-one hours back to the Piraeus, but after our experience on the *Limnos*, we had no hesitation in going third class. After all, we reasoned, ten hours of it would be passed on deck in daylight—what was the use of paying for a cabin in which we were liable to be hideously uncomfortable? As well sit up in the covered portion of the third class. It sounded entirely convincing, but, again, we were wrong.

We boarded the ship in company with a Greek lady who chatted to us in fluent English, which, she told us, she had picked up by reading English books.

'I have brought,' she confided to us, 'my little cart. I never travel without my cart.'

This odd and opulent habit rather took us aback. 'Oh,' murmured Aileen politely, concealing her astonishment, and glancing round for a sight of the vehicle; while my own fancy toyed with a sedan chair, or a litter, as the only possible vehicle in which to mount those steps.

'My little cart is in there,' went on the lady, touching a basket at her feet—and light broke upon us.

'Ah,' I exclaimed involuntarily, and I fear tactlessly, 'your cat.'

She looked at me doubtfully. 'Cat?' she echoed sceptically,

and it was plain she had doubts as to whether my English was not, in a different sense to Chaucer's French, of the Stratford-atte-Bow type! We were travelling deck, were perhaps a little disreputable in appearance, and might well be the possessors of an undesirable accent. Soon she left for the luxury of the second class.

For us, it was at first a journey of which to dream, past Skaros, and the rose-red cliffs of Oia, which are indeed perhaps half as old as Time, and which hold one in a precarious suspension of disbelief; and so on to the island of Ios. Here a few white Venetian-style buildings blossomed like a small plump of mushrooms on the shore of a magnificent harbour, which has rightly gained for the island the title of the Malta of the Aegean. Dominated by Mount Pyrgos, on the slopes of which is the reputed tomb of Homer, it lingers in my mind, like the majority of these island ports, as a dazzle of blue and white—the national colours of Greece.

Steaming north in a blaze of sunshine, the *Despina* reached Naxos in the afternoon, where we were able to watch again that amusing interlude of Harlequin Dabbs, the Voluble Partner, and the Resigned Passengers. From Naxos the boat went across to Paros; by the time we left there, the day was growing dark and cold, and we went down to the covered deck.

We saw at a glance that we had left it too late. Every available inch was littered with bodies, prone whenever possible; and any corner not occupied by them was piled high with chattels. There was everything. Enormous wooden boxes, bulging suitcases, holdalls, paper parcels in every degree of disintegration, and a variety of objects that disdained to travel incognito, crated or wrapped, but flaunted themselves openly—live chickens, the carcase of a great fish attached to a length of string, a gory slab of raw meat, a life-size doll. . . . It looked hopeless, but we were chilled, and edged in warily, treading as delicately as we could amid the human litter. We had left two suitcases on a bench; one had been taken down, but to our joy the other was still there, and we were able to squeeze ourselves into the gap it had kept. And there, on those infernal wooden slats, we sat for the next eleven hours.

The Greeks, ever restless and noisy, were also as ever friendly. There was an uproar of talk and laughter; and we were brought into it with kindly remarks and questions. The seller of loukoúmi, or Turkish delight, who sat opposite to us, was a wag, and continually chaffed his neighbour, an elderly peasant, inviting us with winks to share in the joke. We did our best to look knowing and amused; but in fact we were neither— nor did I think the peasant was particularly entertained. He said little, and spat frequently.

With great difficulty we managed to get sandwiches and Nescafé from a counter at one end of the room. We appeared, however, to be the only people eating, except for the old lady sitting next to me, who had a bag of sweets, which she offered to us with a friendly smile. There was perhaps a general feeling that to take food would be tempting Providence!

We endeavoured to settle down. The place was stuffy, with a fine conglomerate of smells in which the reek of stale tobacco was dominant. After about an hour, I got up to search for a lavatory, and managed by careful manœuvring to reach the companion-way that plumbed the depths. Having descended this hopefully, and tried all the likely-looking doors, I found eventually the filthy and stinking abomination that did duty presumably for all the deck passengers. After I had picked my way back, Aileen set off on the same quest, equipped with full directions, and a solemn warning of the horror that awaited her. She told me on her return that, opening the door of the lavatory and hesitating a moment to rally her nerves, she had been waved in encouragingly by a friendly sailor, who had been watching her with interest from the end of the passage.

Time went on; people, for no reason we could see, stumbled up and down the encumbered gangway in front of our bench, and fell with depressing regularity over our feet. The room became stuffier; the slats began to bite into us. The old lady next to me sank into slumber, so did the soldier on the other side of Aileen; here and there someone snored; but we found it impossible to sleep; I wondered if we would have done better to follow the example of a young German, who had come on board with us at Santorin, and who was sleeping on deck in one of the life-saving rafts. But he had a sleeping-bag; and anyway, he told us later it was extremely hard lying, and he hadn't slept.

Suddenly, the butt of the loukoúmi seller decided he had had enough: he wrapped his head completely in a blanket, and relaxed. This decisive gesture of withdrawal was a slight damper, and talk, at least in our neighbourhood, died away; but everyone fidgeted. The men with komboloi—those strings of beads that have no religious significance but serve as something with which to fiddle—clicked them incessantly; and those without komboloi twiddled their key-chains. People still moved around, and over our feet. Conversation still went on.

Fidgeting myself, and looking about me, I became aware of the plight of a young married couple. She had lain down earlier on a rug in the middle of the room, but he had been late in returning from the deck; and when he did come in, the human tide had cut her off, and she was completely marooned in a sea of recumbent forms. He hesitated, but it was plainly impossible to reach her without treading on someone. He waved sadly to her, and presently went away; but again and again during the night he came back to see that all was well, and to sigh as Troilus sighed toward the Grecian tents where Cressid lay.

All through the night there were sporadic outbursts of talk and movement; and hour after hour we turned and twisted on our wooden grill. There were times when we dozed for a few minutes, to wake with a start as some particular ache made itself felt; but mostly we sat stoically enduring our discomfort. The one thing for which we were profoundly thankful was a sea like glass that brought no qualms to the susceptible Greeks.

△ Plate X NAXOS. *Naxos Town*

▽ Plate XI KYTHNOS. *Castle*

△ Plate XII KYTHNOS. *Our guide at Vriocastro*

△ Plate XIII SERIPHOS. *Livadhi Harbour*

▽ Plate XIV SERIPHOS. Upper Town

△ Plate XV SIPHNOS. *Kastron*

△ Plate XVI SIPHNOS. The Chrysostomos

△ Plate XVII MELOS. *Alley in Citadel*

△ Plate XVIII MELOS. *Klima*

▽ Plate XIX MELOS. *Zephyria*

It was soon after five o'clock in the morning when a stir ran through our company; and a cry went up:

'Piraeus! Piraeus!'

In a moment everyone was scrambling to their feet—as excited and as congratulatory as though we had been untold months at sea, or had just escaped a deadly peril.

'*Thálassa! Thálassa!*' exclaimed Aileen joyfully; and if inaccurate, it was certainly appropriate, for I was prepared to swear the Ten Thousand had been no more relieved to reach the sea than we to reach the land.

Twenty minutes later, we stepped on to the quay in a cold, misty dawn, and were mobbed by the porters of the Piraeus.

◁ Plate XX PAROS. Paroikia. Castle

Chapter Nine

KYTHNOS

The Haunted Castle

IT was on a later occasion that we made our way to the Western Cyclades. On the day before we were due to sail we went down to the Piraeus, and endeavoured to find where our ship, the *Kephallenia*, would berth; but although a clerk in a shipping office on the quay, after conferring doubtfully with his colleagues, did indicate a spot, it was obviously a good-hearted but reckless attempt to send us away happy. In which it failed.

The Piraeus is a disappointment, with little to recall its ancient glory. It suggests a compound of Manchester and Margate, of drab commercialism and Skylark frolics. The noisy, dusty front, with its ancient, racketty trams, its motley of dingy buildings and mean little shops, its uneven, badly-laid pavement, has an air of early-industrial squalor; but much of the harbour makes a gay appearance. It is given over to passenger and pleasure craft, to boats touring the islands, cruise steamers, and a multitude of ferries plying to Aegina and Salamis, while one part of the front is as thick as any holiday-resort promenade with ticket touts offering excursions to Hydra and Poros.

I believe there are a few classical fragments hidden away in the waste of buildings, but we have never made an effort to find them, and on this occasion we fled back to Athens, where one can at least take refuge from the noise by ascending to the Acropolis, or, as we did, by sauntering in the ruins of Hadrian's library and the Roman agora.

Next morning at 9.15, in broiling sunshine, we went down to catch our boat. As usual there was no unanimity among the authorities as to the time it would leave: the reception clerk at the hotel, who made the booking, said 2 p.m.; the people in the office on the quay had been firm that it was 12 noon— so we allowed a wide margin of safety. Taught by experience, we left our suitcases at the hotel, and carried only rucksacks, which incidentally enabled us to travel down to the Piraeus on the metro. It was a journey through a district that appeared to be in a melancholy condition of arrested development, to be going up or coming down without attaining finality in either direction, so that nothing could be seen but tottering remains or rising skeletons, amid a chaotic clutter of bricks and rubble and debris of all kinds.

There was no sign of the *Kephallenia* when we reached the appointed spot; we made further inquiries, and were directed to a distant quay—and told to hurry! We hurried; and about 10.15 we found her, and went aboard.

Two hours passed.

The little ferries phuttered in and out; a diver cleaned his rubber suit, and finally went down in it—on what business we could not guess; a few passengers arrived, and the vendor of soft drinks did a good trade, for it was swelteringly hot. There drifted to us the pungent smell of the charred meat on the spits in the open-air braziers of the tavernas.

About 1.15 the *Kephallenia* prepared to sail, and began to cast off her hawsers. At which moment, a number of intending passengers, who had accepted the 2 p.m. schedule with touching faith, arrived on the quay.

There was a fine clamour.

A single hawser from the stern yet remained attached to the quay; and over the stern, hoisted by their friends and hauled across the gunwale by the sailors, the newcomers were brought aboard, in a high state of agitation.

The hawser was cast off; we drew away—just as a gentleman on the quay became aware he still held a packet of sandwiches for one of the passengers. With desperate courage, he hurled the packet across the widening gap. Alas, it hit below the gunwale, and went to the fishes; but we sailed out with a fine blazon of egg and tomato on the port quarter!

It was 1.30!

Since we would reach our destination at Kythnos before dark, we were travelling deck once more; and grateful for the breeze we now received, we sat, and watched the Attic coast glide by for the next three hours. About 4 p.m., Sunion came into view, and we saw against the sky the columns of the temple of Poseidon that crown the rocky headland. It was these columns, the last glimpse of home for the Greek mariner plying between the Piraeus and the Levant, which led to its being called Cape Colonna in the old days. Here it was that in 1750 the ship *Britannia*, bound from Alexandria to Venice, was driven by a violent storm. Her second mate was William Falconer, and he has described what happened.

> But now Athenian mountains they descry,
> And o'er the surge Colonna frowns on high;
> Where marble columns, long by time defaced,
> Moss-covered on the lofty Cape are placed.

But:

> The circling beach in murderous form appears,
> Decisive goal of all their hopes and fears:
> The seamen now in wild amazement see
> The scene of ruin rise beneath their lee.

In vain they attempt to claw off the Cape—

> The ship hangs hovering on the verge of death,
> Hell yawns, rocks rise, and breakers roar beneath!

At last:

> Ah Heaven!—behold her crashing ribs divide!
> She loosens, parts, and spreads in ruin o'er the tide.[1]

Falconer and two others escaped from the wreck; and this obscure Scottish youth, who was almost entirely self-educated, subsequently wrote the poem on his experience, from which the above lines are taken. He called it The Shipwreck, and it brought him fame.

Byron, who visited Sunion on the 23rd January 1810, and scratched his initials on one of the pillars, was an admirer of Falconer, and referred to 'the infinite superiority of Falconer's "Shipwreck" over all other shipwrecks'.[2] It is in fact still very readable. Falconer, although he was at one time offered a partnership by John Murray, the publisher, stuck to the sea, and after all, he was born to be drowned, for he went down in 1770 with the frigate Aurora in the Mozambique Channel.

The light was beginning to fade when we arrived off Port Mérikha on Kythnos. Situated on the east shore of a narrow and fairly deep inlet surrounded by low hills, the tiny port had a pretty, amateurish air about it, as though it were trying hard to be business-like but cheerfulness had broken in. There was a small jetty, and beyond this a curving strip of sand with, behind it, a few tamarisk trees and a thin scattering of houses: a caique moored to the jetty lent an authentic touch, but somehow, coloured umbrellas and deck-chairs on the sand would have been more in character.

Quite a number of people were rowed ashore with us, and we were fortunate in encountering a young Greek who spoke a little English, and who was going our way to the Chora, or capital village, of the island. He explained that there was a taxi, but that, owing to a mistake, it had gone to meet the boat at Loutra, the other port; no doubt it would soon be here. Meantime, we must sit and drink coffee with him.

Darkness fell, and about half an hour later the taxi trundled shakily on to the quay. Quite often in remote parts of Greece one comes across magnificent taxis, scintillating, opulent machines that appear as improbable as if some local fairy-godmother had created them out of pumpkins; but this one, while not decrepit, had a tired look. It was an average size with room for one beside the driver, and five, at a pinch, in the back. There were already two people in front, not including the driver, who had walked away. We got in at the back, followed by two men, one of whom carried a large framed picture. Our friend joined us, and the car was now full—but in Greece a car is never full while a passenger is left. Somehow, with the greatest difficulty, two more men inserted themselves —and we were seven in the back. Now indeed we felt the pinch. It was impossible to move hand or foot, and every moment I expected the glass of the picture to shatter over us. And then, with relentless determination, another man bored his way in, and lay uneasily on our packed bodies.

Breathing became difficult.

At last the driver took his seat, bringing a young girl with him—and presently the old car slowly and laboriously gathered way, and crept up the hill from the port, with a grand total aboard of twelve!

All the same, once up the hill, she almost careered along: that is to say, I estimated she was doing close on ten miles an hour, which, in the circumstances, was quite reckless. For Aileen, who was better wedged for looking out of the window, declared the road had as many artificial impediments as it had of the humps and cavities that are congenital with nearly all Greek roads. The latter I knew all about, because the jolts from them, added to the pressure we were under, nearly winded me; but every now and then, there would come a violent swerve, which was even more rib-crushing, and this, Aileen reported, was due to a mound of sand, or a heap of stones, that would loom out of the darkness in the very centre of the fairway, where it had been left, apparently, for the greater convenience of a road gang.

It was the longest five kilometres I have ever known; and when we arrived at the Chora, and I crawled out, taking deep breaths, I felt myself gradually expand like an inflating balloon. Aileen, who had somehow managed to keep to the top layer of stratified humanity, was not quite so battered; and by some miracle the picture also emerged intact—revealing itself in the car lights as a portrait of the King of Greece.

We were led to a tiny hotel in the village, where the landlady showed us into a room already occupied by an elderly Greek: it was plain she intended to turn him out. We protested vigorously, and retreated in a hurry, but no-one paid any attention; the occupant, quite unruffled, folded his garments and silently stole away to another room, and we were ushered in again, feeling horribly privileged and ashamed!

The Chora by daylight emerged as a long, straggling village of little more than one street. Some of the buildings had a medieval air, and probably dated back to Venetian times; but the medieval feature that impressed us most were the cobbles: at the north, by the tiny *platea* and town hall, the pavement was good, but at the opposite end were great knobbly stones that were appallingly uncomfortable to walk on, especially at night, when, there being little public lighting, one had to take them blind.

On that first morning we made a new friend, George Ayiopetrides, who came across and introduced himself to us while we were at breakfast. George was the local miller, a brown, wiry little man, who was over eighty years old, but looked twenty years younger and slung his flour sacks around as though he were. He spoke excellent English, not to mention German and Russian, for he had spent many years in England —living not a stone's throw from our own home in London. He took us to his house, where he was particularly proud of the bathroom, which he had built with his own hands two years before, when a new water system on the island had made this possible. It looked most efficient, and I congratulated him. He nodded; then with twinkling eyes, and exploding with inward laughter at a joke he felt sure an Englishman would appreciate, he said: 'But I have never used it—I am too lazy!'

He was indeed always bubbling with amusement: he had lost most of the money he had made abroad, when the drachma crashed; his mill was no longer paying; it was heavy work for him, and for his wife, who helped him; but nothing had subdued the cheerful spirit of 'Mr Potatoes'—as the Londoners had called him.

We were anxious to try and reach the remains of a Venetian castle on the north coast of the island; and having received directions from George, we started soon after ten o'clock.

Kythnos, or Thermia—or Fermene to the Venetians—has an almost unbroken connection of nearly three hundred years with the Gozzadini. A part of the original Duchy of Sanudo, it was ravaged in 1292 by the Aragonese admiral, Roger de Lluria, who was ostensibly fighting the Byzantine Greeks, but who plundered everything within reach. In 1323 Niccolò I Sanudo gave Kythnos to the Castelli, a middle-class nouveau-riche family, who were looked down upon by the very exclusive island aristocracy; but thirteen years later, the Gozzadini, with the tacit approval of Niccolò, took it from them. Except for a brief interval of five years when the Duchy fell to the Turks, Kythnos remained with the Gozzadini until 1617.

In the Second World War a Long Range Desert Group party was landed on the island, and despite the presence of a German occupying force, it remained there in hiding for several weeks, sending back by wireless valuable reports of enemy shipping movements. It was something of an achievement, for Kythnos is not a particularly easy island on which to hide.[3]

Tournefort had another disturbed night in a chapel here, for the country folk took his party for corsairs, and at three in the morning, armed men broke into the chapel. Whereupon, as he, or rather his translator, elegantly puts it: 'When we had satisfied them, they told us, that had it not been for the prudent Remonstrances of the Consul of France, we had gone to pot, every Mother's Son of us.' [4]

It took us between three and four hours to reach the castro. At first we followed the excellent road that leads north from the Chora down the ridge to the port of Loutra—where are the celebrated hot springs, for which a bathing house was erected in the reign of King Otho. Theodore Bent took a very poor view of Loutra: 'Not a tree near, and a hideous waste of sand, impregnated with mineral water, between the bathhouse and the sea; rheumatism for life would be preferable to a month of the burning summer spent here.'⁵ That is a little strong, I think; but I have to confess that we only went within a few hundred yards of Loutra, being too anxious to push on to our castle. From where we turned off, Loutra certainly looked a rather bare sprawl of buildings, but it had an attractive situation on its inlet among low hills. There was indeed no tree to be seen, but that is typical of Kythnos, which creates the general impression of a naked, good-for-nothing island, burnt with sun, scaly with rock, and barren as sea-sand. But in fact this is not fair to it. It is hardly a very fertile island, but, walking from the Chora, we had found, in the hollows, olives, figs, lemons and giant reeds; a little corn had been grown on terraces, there were vines, and a few root crops. Nor were flowers altogether wanting; here and there a dog onion pushed up a white plume, a form of lentisk, or *schínos*, was displaying red berries, and there was no overlooking the lesser elecampane with its yellow flowers and its strong and revolting smell.

We turned off the road into a dry watercourse, and found a track that led over the hills to the north of Loutra. Here we encountered a party of locals, bringing down donkeys with a load of thorn bushes for fuel. The men told us the castro was not far, and waved a hand vaguely northward; but it took us nearly a couple of hours to find it. We were brought up short at last by coming to the end of the island, the northern point of Cape Kephalos, where we had a fine view of Kea, Andros, Tenos, and, in the distance, the hills above Kárystos, but could not see a sign of any castle in our vicinity.

Returning rather disconsolately, we had passed the abandoned monastery of St George, lying in a dip about half a mile back, when Aileen spotted what might be a wall on the skyline to the west of the Cape. We made for it—and there, well camouflaged, was our castle.

It is finely situated, much like Skaros, on a peninsula of rock, five hundred feet high, joined to the shore by a narrow isthmus. (Plate XI) Approaching from the east across the isthmus, one sees to the best advantage the only intact feature, a tall, square tower defending the gateway. A low wall runs from it, through which passes, via a ragged arch, the present path to the summit of the rock. Here there is a modern chapel, and, a little farther west, the ruins of a rectangular hall built in modern times with old materials; all else on the rock, with the exception of a small vaulted chapel with faint frescoes, is in utter ruin—a desolation of broken-down walls, a huge shattering of masonry lying amid the thick, tussocky grass, the thistles and the clumps of spiny burnet. The debris is spread over the whole rock, but in places it has been built into lengths of drystone walling, presumably by shepherds as a rude fold—or maybe these are relics of the time, in 1821, when the islanders took refuge here from the Turks.

In this wreckage one can do no more than trace the remains of a cistern, the broken steps leading down to a choked well, the foundation of a tower or the angle of a redoubt. It is a spot both melancholy and disconcerting: the tower, viewed as one approaches the castle, has a stern air that brings one to a respectful halt, picturing a massive concentration of power behind it on that sheer and narrow rock. But beyond the façade, one steps out of the illusion so abruptly as to be startled and depressed, confronted with the ugly frailty of human achievement; for, unlike the Apanocastro at Naxos, there is in this scrap-heap no recognizable lineament of the proud and vigorous life that once flourished here. I could well believe that the people of Kythnos have always regarded it as haunted. Here, indeed, the shades when they gather must have a double cause for wailing, since, returning to sorrow over the place they loved, they find that it, too, has now vanished.

The other site on Kythnos is that of the classical town at Vriocastro. It is on the west coast, just above the curve of Episcopi Bay, which is the inlet directly north of Port Mérikha, and there is a mule track to it that branches off about three-quarters of the way down the road from the Chora to the port. George had persuaded a friend of his to act as guide, and next day the three of us took the taxi as far as the track.

Our guide, Constantine Glukoyianis, was the most picturesque figure we had met in Greece. (Plate XII) A veteran of the
Balkan War of 1912, in which he had been twice wounded,
he was every bit as handsome and as martial as our Filla
friend, but where the latter had been gravely dignified, this
old moustache had the gay, careless swagger of the true
palikari. Dressed in a blue jacket with red stripes, which Aileen
coveted, with a straw hat held by a chinstrap at the back of his
head like a halo, with faded blue jeans, and sandals which he
called *thorákia*, made of strips of old motor-tyre laced to the
foot by cords over the instep, he sauntered ahead, crooning a
plaintive little song of which I could only catch the words
'*agápe mou*' ('my love').

Half an hour's walk brought us to Vriocastro. There is not
much to be seen: the sites of the theatre and the acropolis, a
few feet of classical wall, dry and ashlar faced—and three
caves cut out of the rock, side by side, which Bent thought
might have been a Roman reservoir.

There is, however, a grand view along the coast, with two
deep bays, one on each side, between which, directly opposite,
is the tiny, haunted islet of Vriocastraki. Once called Daskaleio,
this was the place to which were brought, after being exhumed
from their tombs on the main island, the remains of those
dead who in the opinion of the natives were given to the
unpleasant habit of 'walking'. Here they were re-buried, and
the living were then able to heave a sigh of relief, for of course
the 'walkers' were unable to cross water.

Our guide sauntered along, singing happily, or chatting
volubly to us, and in spite of getting no coherent response,
enjoying himself hugely; he had rather the air of a feudal
chieftain conducting guests round his domain—and indeed that turned out to be more or less the fact, for we
gathered that he owned most of the land covered by the
site.

We ate our sandwiches, and took his photograph, on the
ledge before the caves—under a large caper bush whose cool

splash of green on this brown, desiccated upland seemed a miracle akin to the blooming of Aaron's rod.

On our return, we found the Chora humming with activity: the priest was painting the church door; men were touching up fences and walls, and women were renewing the whitewash lines that formed the traditional gridiron pattern on the streets. We learned that next day the King and Queen of Greece were to visit the island. I now saw the reason for the picture that had arrived with us in the taxi.

Everyone had become involved in the upheaval, and the preparations went on far into the night. It was, I fancy, largely a matter of food, and evidently our landlady, Kuría Eiréne, had a leading part in the operation, for, long after we had gone to bed, people were rushing in and out of the hotel, anxiously demanding her. No sooner did we get to sleep than our door was flung open, and we were woken by a cry of 'Eir-éne!', so despairing that but for its human vigour I might have felt my hair rising!

The Royal visitors arrived punctually next day. Children strewed flowers before them; they were entertained by an exhibition of dancing in the *platea*; and were then escorted through the village by everyone—to the thin strains evoked by two fiddlers sawing furiously as they marched.

That night we found our restaurant packed. An orchestra of one fiddle and one mandoline played over and over a single monotonous tune, accompanied at intervals by a few high, nasal voices among the patrons, while two couples in the island dress danced in a cleared space. The dance was largely an opportunity for the man to exhibit his virtuosity; the girl did nothing but pivot slowly and gravely, while he, keeping his distance, revolved with an ebullience that reached a climax when he leapt daringly in the air, clapping his heels together and slapping his thighs. Judging, however, from what I had seen of the same dance in the *platea*, this bit of joie de vivre was not quite in the best tradition.

It was intolerably boring. The heat and the noise were

almost insupportable, though the patrons had a Johnsonian ability to become jovial on lemonade, or at least on beer, for hardly any wine or spirits were being served. Next morning, it is true, when we walked in, the place looked as if there had been an orgy, or as if Circe had been feeding her swine, the tables and floor filthy with gobbets of food and spilt drink—but much of the mess was perhaps accounted for by the Greek tendency to be economical with plates.

After lunch we left for Seriphos. Port Mérikha, bathed in sunlight, looked as frivolously decorative as ever. It was siesta time, not a human being was in sight, but a bottle in a wicker case lay on the abandoned quay as though symbolizing the genial spirit of the place. At about three o'clock our boat arrived, the little port came to life, and at least half a dozen people appeared.

We were rowed out over a popply sea, for there was a strong breeze, and found the boat to be the *Karaiskakês*, the 'fast *Karaiskakês*', as the posters termed her, and in fact she is rather better than most.

Outside the harbour the sea was really choppy, and leaping like the goats from which it was once held that the word 'Aegean' derived. Half-way over, the Pepper-pot, or solitary rock of Pipéri, came into view; a huge perpendicular marble crag, it reminded Aileen of the bow of a great liner sinking by the stern. It offers no landing place, and the *Mediterranean Pilot* says tersely, 'it is inaccessible'.

At the end of two hours, we were running south down the high, rocky eastern coast of Seriphos; but approaching from this direction, we could see nothing of our goal, the Livadhi inlet, until the ship, rounding a tongue of land, turned through almost a half-circle, and we were in the most spectacular harbour I have seen in the Aegean. (Plate XIII)

Chapter Ten

SERIPHOS

The Unspeakable Adoldo

I N front of us, at the head of the inlet, a pyramidal hill rose
steeply, as clean and pointed in outline as though it were a
spearhead thrust up by some Titan from the underworld;
and, incredibly, there was a sparkle of white houses up to the
very point. That was the Chora. Even in daylight, it seemed to
hang above us with a touch of fantasy, as of a mirage; and at
night beneath a moon the white streak showed like a cloud
in the sky, so that, knowing what it was, one could scarcely
believe one's eyes. A wall of higher mountains ran behind the
hill of the Chora, like the curtain of a second enceinte raised
by Nature against the human powers that had so daringly
scaled her outer work.

On the left, or western side of the inlet, was the port. It had
much the same lay-out as Port Mérikha—a jetty, and a huddle
of houses fronting a curve of loose sand fringed by tamarisk
trees; but this was a straggling, untidy settlement, whose main
attraction was the gay flotilla of boats moored off it in the
company of two caiques.

There was, I had heard in Athens, an hotel, and I asked the
young Greek who had rowed us ashore if this were so, and
where it was; he waved vaguely. However, I had a letter of
introduction to a Mr Livanios, the 'President' of the island,
who, I eventually discovered, ran the local *pantopoleíon*, or
grocery store. His wife told me he was away, but she handed
us over to an elderly little man who, she affirmed, would take

us to an hotel; he led us to the near end of the village where an empty double-fronted bungalow looked bleakly out to sea. As we reached it, the boatman came up, beaming: 'My father,' he said, indicating our guide, 'will look after you good'— upon which I began to suspect that we had been discreetly inveigled away from the hotel, and into 'Father's' hands.

There is no electricity on Seriphos except where it is generated on the premises, so that it was in semi-darkness that we peered into one of the front rooms of the bungalow. We were able to make out that it had two unmade beds, one table with a tin basin, one chair with an oil lamp, and some pegs on the wall. Father hastened to light the oil lamp, and we were then able to see that the room was dirty, the bare wooden floor littered with cigarette ends, and that a dead crayfish lay on the table.

However, we had expected things to be a bit rough, and I told Father it would do, whereupon he bustled round energetically. Meanwhile I went down the passage, and found a lavatory, in which were also a hand basin and a shower; it stank diabolically, and not a dribble of water flowed from anything. I notified Father. He was incredulous. Of course there was water. He hurried to the lavatory, turned on the tap, and registered stunned amazement.

Immediately he became even more furiously active. He ran outside, and disinterred a long hose with which he endeavoured to fill the roof tank of the bungalow from a tap on the front. It was no good: every time he turned on the tap, the hose blew off. He was alternately patient, exasperated, and grimly determined; and it became a performance that was irresistibly funny to watch. In the end he succeeded, filled the tank, beckoned me to follow him, and turned on the tap in the lavatory. A thin trickle came out. He regarded me with touching complacency. I looked at the lavatory cistern, and back at him inquiringly. At that, he shook his head sadly: then, raising his eyebrows, hunching his shoulders, spreading his hands, he made it clear that nothing short of the rod of Moses could draw water from that cistern. A pantomime that somehow managed to convey also his confidence that, as a man of the world, I would appreciate the unimportance of this trifle. One could not help feeling rather drawn to him!

Aileen and I went out to hunt for food, and had walked the length of the waterfront, when there burst upon us in a blaze of its own electric light the genuine tourist hotel. Feeling rather aggrieved, we went in, and talked to the manager, who spoke tolerable English. The hotel, we found, was on the point of closing for the season, and although I think he might have offered us accommodation, he would not provide a meal. Where could we eat? 'I believe,' he replied, with a magnificent affectation of aloofness from the paltry affairs of the village, 'I believe there is a restaurant attached to the hotel you are in.' Not much attracted by his manner, and remembering the charm of Father, we felt reconciled to our austere room and hard beds.

With some difficulty we located the restaurant on the front. It was the typical bare, cavernous room, lit here by calor gas, which provided the white glare of an incandescent mantle; there were the normal high ceiling, glass-sided counter, and dim, blotched advertisements—all contriving to remind me of one of those ancient, morgue-like railway waiting-rooms. But here was the added gaiety of a cuckoo-clock; and the proprietor, who welcomed us with the smile of an old friend, was, of course, Father!

We came to like the little man immensely. He was friendly, full of good spirits, and nothing was too much trouble for him. Seriphos is a poor island, meat and potatoes were scarce, and the food in his restaurant was confined mainly to whatever fish could be had at the moment; nor was his cooking up to much—soups and vegetables were unfailingly lukewarm— but fortunately he had eggs, and this made up for a great deal.

We started early the following morning to explore the Chora. (Plate XIV) It takes about forty minutes to reach the top of the hill, and, particularly at the end, it is an exciting walk, climbing up steep lanes among houses that teeter on the lip of a crag. The buildings, however, do not close in on one as they do at Naxos, and all the way up there are lovely views over the harbour, to the open sea, and the little island of Vous. At the Chora we contacted a Greek who spoke French, and who came round with us, fortifying himself with glasses of the local wine for the attack on the summit.

Seriphos was noted in antiquity as the island to which Danäe and her son, Perseus, floated in the chest in which they had been set adrift by her father. Iron was discovered quite early on the island, and it has never ceased to be mined there, except during the Second World War. So rich is it in iron ore that in the seventeenth century shipmasters were known to complain that the island deflected their compass needles. When the Venetians arrived in the Aegean, Seriphos, known to them as 'Serfento', was taken by Andrea and Geremia Ghisi, aided by Dominico Michieli and Pietro Giustiniani; and the island was divided among the four. Seventy years later, Licario, the renegade, with a Greek fleet captured it, and it remained Greek until just before the turn of the century, when the same three families recovered it.

It was in a dreadful state, having been continually raided by pirates; for the Byzantine Greeks had been unable to protect it. Its Venetian castles, built in the first occupation, were in ruins, and its towns almost abandoned, because the inhabitants preferred to live permanently in hiding in the mountains.[1] In 1355 half of Seriphos was granted to the Venetian, Ermolao Minotto, who, by his liberal administration of the iron mines, brought a golden age to Seriphos. The island became one of the most important places in the Cyclades; and many of the serfs working in the mines were able to save enough money to buy their freedom. Then, as the century drew to its end, there came the appalling régime of Minotto's successor, Niccolò Adoldo.

An absentee landlord, Adoldo left the management of the mines to a deputy, and only visited the island to collect his dues; but these visits were a nightmare to the inhabitants. His sole desire was to extract money, and he and his deputy were utterly unscrupulous, ignoring the rights of the workers, and compelling them to submit to blatant injustice; nor did he pay much attention to the mining rights vested in the Michieli and Giustiniani families.

The climax was reached one day in 1393.

Adoldo arrived in the island accompanied by a bodyguard of Cretan thugs. He held his usual levée, extorted all the money he could, and, for once, declared himself satisfied. More than that, he invited the notables of the island to dine with him, in the castle on the summit of the Chora hill. They accepted, but as soon as they had gathered at the castle, Adoldo gave a signal, and his bodyguard closed round them. Adoldo then declared that he knew they had concealed much of their wealth from fear of himself, but that he was determined to get it; and each guest was bound and subjected to torture to make him confess the whereabouts of his money. There is some difference of opinion as to whether or not Adoldo obtained confessions, but there is no doubt about the sequel—every guest was flung to his death from the castle cliff on to the rocks below.

It was too much even for that brutal age.

When at last the news reached Venice, Adoldo was accused before the Senate by the Michieli and Giustiniani, and was found guilty. He was condemned to two years rigorous imprisonment, his share of Seriphos was confiscated, and he was forbidden to return to the island. A punishment, one feels, that well reflects the attitude of that privileged society to its subject people. Miller adds that 'he died at a ripe old age in the odour of sanctity; his remains were interred in the church of S. Simeone Piccolo, which he endowed, and a splendid tomb was erected over his unworthy ashes'.[2] This is the church that every visitor emerging from the railway station at Venice sees confronting him across the Grand Canal.

In a short time the island passed entirely into the hands of the Michieli, who held it until 1536, when Barbarossa, intent on picking up galley-slaves and gold, made his famous swoop on the islands. He took Seriphos, and it never went back to the Venetians.

There is very little left of the castle. At the highest point of the hill is a rocky platform on which the keep formerly stood: the remains of two square towers, one below the other, which were presumably once part of the defences here, have been converted into chapels, and the only other relic on the summit is a stone reservoir of great age, in which an odd, pinkish cement, whose constituents are unknown, has been used. On the north of this platform, the side away from the harbour, the cliff falls nearly sheer, needing no fortifications, and it was here, no doubt, that Adoldo's victims were flung down. The town lies on the gentler slopes to south and west, and one can see some indications of the walls that once bounded two enceintes, the lower of which has on the west an unpretentious doorway that marks the main gate.

It is, however, near the summit, in narrow alleys between the remaining lengths of old wall, that one gets the feel of a citadel; and here, too, are the arms of the Michieli—a shield bearing six rows of roundels, with six in the top row, five in the next, and so on to the last row with a single roundel, the whole forming an inverted triangle. There is a story attached to these roundels, which are in fact coins, and commemorate no feat of arms but an expedient adopted by the great Doge Domenico Michiel in the twelfth century. Being in command of a Venetian fleet at the siege of Tyre, he found himself, like many another commander of the past, with no money to pay his men; so he issued them with stamped leather discs, and gave his personal guarantee that these would be exchanged for money when the fleet returned to Venice. The promise was kept, and ever afterward the arms of the Michieli bore seven fesses, azure and argent, having on them twenty-one coins.

Below the shield on either side is a capital M, above is the date 1433, the time when the Michieli took over the whole island. But the arms have been rather poorly placed; for the stone on which they are cut had fallen, and it has been re-erected in a whitewashed wall above the doorway to an outside passage of a house, and is topped by an absurd gable-like stone, so that the whole looks more like a freakish modern decoration than a medieval relic.

The hill of the Chora is connected to the higher mountains behind it by a ridge on the north-west, crowned by a line of windmills; and along this we proceeded next day to find the ancient fortified monastery of the Archangel, which lies over the mountains, on the north-east coast. It was a scorching day, and this corner of Seriphos, shut in by a mountain wall that forms a giant reflector for the sun, is notorious for the way it stokes up. The mule track was particularly stony, and looking at the steep ridge ahead, we realized we were in for a strenuous day. But we had decided to walk for reasons of economy, since a taxi, using the road, would have cost us 150 drachmae merely to take us to the monastery, leaving us to walk back, while mules there and back would have been 200 drachmae.

The track grew stonier and steeper, the day hotter, as we began to worm our way up the mountain face, on which the earth had a reddish tinge as though it were smouldering with the heat. Clumps of spiny burnet dotted it, and there were ranks of withered thistles, still menacing in death, but the only thing we met that looked neither sullen nor moribund was some rest-harrow, defiantly flaunting pink pea-like flowers—that and a large greenish-white butterfly, whose energetic flutterings in the heat provoked Aileen to envy! Now and again a rumble came from the valley, where one of the few iron mines left in operation was being worked, but other-wise there was no sound except the crunch and slither of our boots; not even a cicada chirped. The air is so dry in Greece that one rarely sweats a great deal, but today I was dissolving like a jellyfish on the beach. But Aileen, ever since she had found the rest-harrow, had become oblivious to discomfort, searching eagerly for any other weed that, valiant as Satan in Pandemonium, had raised its standard in this hell.

It was two hours before we got over the ridge. Then we found ourselves looking into a wide valley from a point where a branch track led off to the right, while the main path wound on to a village we were unable to identify. We had only a vague idea of where the monastery was, and we hesitated. In such a dilemma, when one is quite at a loss, there is nothing better to do than to follow the famous advice given to the Duc de Sully by his valet, and to turn to the right—and this we did. The track was hardly more than a ruckle of stones down the hillside, but in about a quarter of an hour it emerged on to a genuine road, or rather to the trail of ruts and potholes that does for a road in these parts.

It went on interminably, curving round the lip of a great bowl in the hills, on its way to the coast; but on this side of the mountains it was cooler, with a light breeze, and the road was a relief after the ankle-twisting mule track. It was one o'clock, and we had been walking for just four hours, when we topped a rise, and caught sight of the monastery.

Standing on a high plateau about a mile from the sea, it looks like a fort, and it is a fort, built to be defended against pirates, with prodigiously thick walls in which almost the only openings are loopholes. The door, on the west, reached by a narrow flight of twelve steps, is barely five feet high, and is protected by a huchette above. It gives on to a porch running through the thickness of the wall to steps that lead down into the central enclosure, most of which is occupied by the church.

From within, the wall of the enclosure is seen to be built in three tiers: an arcade and a line of cells at ground level, a flat terrace above, from which opens an upper row of cells, and above this, a true wall-walk behind a parapet.

As we entered, we found three monks working on a large cistern to the right of the steps. A trifle flustered by our arrival, they hurriedly summoned a colleague to deal with the situation. This was a handsome young man with blue eyes, brown hair, and a fine beard, who looked, I thought, absurdly like an Englishman; and I was not surprised when he told us later that his mother was English. Yet the odd thing was that he either had no English at all, or for some peculiar reason would not speak it. He was, however, most hospitable, entertaining us with cherry jam, water and ouzo in his cell on the second storey.

He had been born in Seriphos, had lived in the monastery for ten years, and had eleven brothers and a sister, whose photographs, with those of his parents, hung in a large frame on the wall. Most of his brothers were in the armed forces, and no doubt it was a very proper arrangement that there should be one man of peace in this martial family. He was quiet, rather shy, but quick to smile, and not without a percipient look in his blue eyes; and though he attended upon us with admirable good manners, I suspected he was tolerantly amused by two people who could find nothing better to do than wander frivolously about the earth: indeed, before we left, I began to feel exactly as though we were children trespassing on the time of a good-natured adult.

There is some doubt about the date the monastery was founded, but the best authorities put it at around 1600, when refugees from Cyprus, which had fallen to the Turks in 1570, came here, bringing with them the ikon of St Michael, from which the monastery gets its name.[3] The church was only completed in 1659. It has an attractive interior, with a fine gold-embellished screen, and a number of lively frescoes by Emmanuel Skordule, a painter-priest from Crete, which depict with vigorous relish the horrors of hell.[4]

Our friend showed us out of the monastery with the final injunction to take our walk back 'sigá! sigá!' ('slowly! slowly!').

Observing this admonition carefully, we had walked for about an hour when we met a nice-looking girl who addressed us in reasonable English. Walking on with us, she chatted freely, and told us a good deal about herself. It was rather a sad story.

Her name was Zaphe, and she had worked for seven years

with an American family in Athens; then she had come back
to Seriphos, and married a miner. But the mines were doing
badly; one by one they were closing, and Zaphe's husband
had been out of work for two years. If they went to Athens
they could earn adequate wages, but neither of them wanted
to leave Seriphos.

Zaphe had a small house at the nearby village of Pyrgos,
where she owned three cows; but she and her husband lived
with his sister in the Chora, and every morning Zaphe did
that gruelling walk over the mountains from the Chora to
Pyrgos to look after her cows.

She had no children, and of course, Greek as she was, she
felt this deeply; but in the early years of her married life she
had had a miscarriage, and now they were so poor that she
could not give up work, and children were out of the question.
I discreetly refrained from asking why the husband didn't
look after the cows—no doubt in Greece this would have been
beneath his dignity.

She was a very likable person, intelligent, frank, and as
devoid of shyness as she was of self-pity, for she was quite
matter-of-fact about her troubles. It was simply how things
were. She had gained a certain poise from her contact with the
American family, which, added to her cheerful, unaffected
manner, made for considerable charm; and in those comparatively few minutes, she took us into her life, and created an atmosphere not only friendly but intimate. Nor was she entirely
absorbed in her own affairs, but was eager to learn about us.

Presently, guiding us by a short cut, she led us up the hillside to where a spring had been piped into a large concrete
basin to form a communal washing centre—an unexpected
amenity on Seriphos, where water is scarce. At this moment
the island's taxi came along the road below, making for the
monastery, and Zaphe suggested we might like to take it on
its return. We were overjoyed at the chance of getting off the
stones, and she went leaping like a goat down the hill to
arrange it with the driver.

On the outskirts of Pyrgos we came on Zaphe's cousin Nick, barefooted, with his trousers rolled to his knees, treading out the grapes—a messy occupation, the stems and skins of the grapes making a thick scum in which he trampled energetically, ankle-deep, sending a thin trickle of juice into a lower basin. In the village we were introduced to Nick's parents, and there was much chatter and laughter all round; but it was plainly a poverty-stricken village, and life there must have been as hard as anywhere in the Aegean, which is saying a good deal.

Yet poverty is not such a misery on these islands as it is in north-western Europe. The sun provides comfort and even entertainment, and existence is not cramped by a mean house, for it is lived mostly out of doors; the weather can be relied on by the tiller of the soil, which lightens his burden; and then, too, in these more primitive island communities the lack of money does not make a great difference in the standard of living, because the extra amenities to be had by the better-off are few. On this view one might well prefer poverty on barren, stony Seriphos to comparative affluence in Athens, where the peace and freedom and friendliness of the island could scarcely be had; though no doubt Zaphe and her husband were chiefly influenced by sentiment and family attachment.

She and a friend came back in the taxi with us. It was good to take the weight off our feet, but nevertheless we had an exhausting journey; most of the time the car was not travelling more than five or six miles an hour, reeling and staggering, cracking down on its springs, or lifting itself with a snarl out of potholes. We were thoroughly shaken, and it might well, I imagine, be said of the Seriphos taxi as of Gay's coach,

> Who can recount the taxi's various harms,
> The legs disjointed, and the broken arms?

But fortunately we arrived in one piece. We were charged only forty drachmae, which seemed modest; and indeed I now began to take a more tolerant view of the 150 drachmae that had been originally asked, for it was difficult to see how the taxi owner made a living when the life of a car on Seriphos was obviously of few days and full of trouble.

We usually had breakfast on the terrace outside Father's café, and almost every morning I had noticed a woman prowling along the shore, past the tamarisk trees, with a gun under her arm. She wore a sombrero, a leather coat, a long skirt and boots, and she reminded me of those Victorian spinsters who treated the world as their parish, and would spend half a lifetime living decorously, in the fashion of a lady of the manor, among cannibals or head-hunters. Sometimes there were one or two men with her, also with guns, and I wondered vaguely what they were after—until one day Father rushed into the restaurant, holding up a dead starling, and crying: 'Aúrion! Aúrion!' ('Tomorrow! Tomorrow!'). I gathered that tomorrow we should feast on the starling. It then dawned on me that the tamarisk trees on the beach were probably the main covert for the sportsmen of Seriphos, and that the lady and her companions had been shooting for the pot. The 'guns' turned out to be air rifles.

Father himself used to go out hopefully to add to the menu; but I believe he was a somewhat emotional sportsman, and, rather in the manner of Mr Brontë, who vented his annoyance by firing pistols from his back door, Father liked to loose off when provoked. I heard that on one occasion, furious at having missed a sitting bird, he took a pot-shot at his neighbour's hen!

Shooting was not his only hobby. On the day after we had visited the monastery, we left Seriphos in the evening; but before we left, Father, as a last token of friendship, brought out his collection of mechanical toys. There were a musical box, an old gentleman who smoked a cigar, and finally, the star turn, an electric cat, working on a battery and having remote control, that walked and flashed its eyes. His pride in these was touching.

At seven o'clock that evening we bought our tickets in Mr

Livanios's shop, and at his wife's invitation sat down to wait for the boat, while the family took their dinner beside us. In spite of my letter of introduction, Mr Livanios had never made himself known to me, and although he was there at the head of his table, he still remained incognito; but, as will be seen, he was not unmindful of our interests.

An interminable hour and a half passed. We replied with flashing smiles to an occasional incomprehensible remark from the family, and tried to relieve the boredom by inspecting the shop. It was extraordinarily well stocked with tinned goods—you would hardly have done better in any round-the-corner grocer in London—owing probably to the demand by visiting yachts, two of which came in while we were on the island.

We had almost fallen into a coma when at last there was a faint hoot that might have been an owl. In a moment, as though it had been an Indian signal, we were all on our feet, and tumbling out into the darkness.

Chapter Eleven

SIPHNOS

The Fair Haven

ONCE again our ship was the *Kephallenia*. It is only about an hour to Siphnos, but, thinking it might be cold, we had taken second-class tickets. Mrs Livanios had sold me these, but for some reason she would not give them to me, but handed them to her husband, who came aboard with us. There he spoke to the chief steward, who presently ushered us into a well-upholstered saloon—so comfortable in fact that I wondered if Livanios had exerted a little influence, and had had us transferred to the first-class. I still don't know. But before he left, I felt we ought to get acquainted. 'Are you George Livanios?' I asked. Emerging reluctantly from his anonymity, he gave me a hurried nod. Upon which, like two conspirators sharing a fateful secret, we shook hands gravely, and parted.

Kamares on Siphnos was no more than a tiny cluster of brilliants hung upon the black throat of an inlet. On shore a bus was waiting, which took us, at a charge of three drachmae each, the four miles to the main village of Apollonia, where we found a tourist hotel, and the best accommodation we had yet enjoyed on these western islands.

Apollonia, and four other villages, all linked with one another, are strung along a ridge running north and south; but our first objective next day was not to explore these, but to make our way to the old Venetian town of Kastron, which was the capital in the time of the Duchy. Occupying the site of the classical town, it is on the east coast about a couple of miles from Apollonia. Below it is the little bay of Kastron, once known as Seralia, and it was here, about the year 525 B.C., that the Samians, who had been in revolt against their tyrant, Polycrates, sailed in to demand gold of the wealthy Siphnians. The bulwarks of the Samian galleys were painted red, according to Herodotus, and thus the Delphic oracle was justified, for it had told the Siphnians to beware of 'a wooden ambush, and a herald in red'.[1] The Samians landed, defeated the Siphnians, and before they left exacted a hundred talents from them. But the Siphnians were well able to afford the money; for their gold and silver mines had rendered them extremely wealthy, as may be gathered from the reputation in ancient times of their treasury at Delphi.

Siphnos was a part of Sanudo's Duchy, but it went back to the Greeks, with so many other islands, when Licario was raiding the Aegean. Then in 1307 another formidable adventurer, this time of Spanish origin, seized it. He was Januli da Corogna, who belonged to the Knights of St John, but who, as soon as he had made his capture, threw off his allegiance to the Order, and declared himself a free and independent sovereign.

About 1465 the island passed to the acquisitive and limpet-like Gozzadini, by the marriage of Niccolò Gozzadini to Margaritta, the da Corogna heiress; and here, as at Kythnos, the Gozzadini régime lasted, with a short break at the fall of the Duchy, until 1617, when Angelo Gozzadini, the last lord, was evicted by the Turks.

It took about forty minutes to walk to Kastron. Siphnos is a fertile island, and the way ran over hills that were everywhere terraced; the terraces were mostly revetted with drystone walling, which allows the water to flow through, and similar walling flanked many of the mule tracks that made a network over the land. The Siphnians seem particularly expert not only at this drystone work, but also at building in a kind of modern variant of cyclopean masonry, in which, although mortar is used, stones of irregular shape appear to be cunningly chiselled to fit more or less together. Here, too, as in other islands, they make use of sun-baked bricks, which are built into walls and then cemented or plastered over.

Eventually our road dropped to the floor of a curving valley between terraced hills, and Kastron came into view about three-quarters of a mile away, on a dome-like hill rising to about a thousand feet above the sea. The white buildings contrasting with the brown earth of the terraces below, and outlined against the sea beyond, had a neat and compact look; for, excepting a few houses lining the approach, Kastron has not, as have most of these old fortified towns, strayed beyond its wall.

The curtain here is really composed of the outside walls of houses that were built on purpose to form this defence. It is in fact a double curtain on the west, where an inner and lower wall runs parallel, made up of one-storey houses—now mainly used as storerooms and warehouses. Between the two is a lane, spanned by the bridges that are a distinctive feature of Kastron; most of them are of stone, but there are a few wooden ones, and they connect the first storey of the outer houses to the roof of the inner ones. (Plate XV) No doubt their purpose was to aid the defence by facilitating communication with the outer wall; while they also enabled the lane to be enfiladed should an enemy penetrate to it.

Like ancient Thebes, Kastron is often reputed to have seven gates, but in fact there are only five, three on the west, and two on the east, facing the sea. The land gates are curious and interesting: reached from the outside by rough steps, each is a vaulted passage, or porch, extending through the thickness of the houses. Originally closed by iron doors, they have stone benches in them, and in addition to their proper function, they served the inhabitants as meeting places in the manner of the ancient stoas, being lighted at night by a great lantern hanging from the roof. They are known as *lózies*; there is the *Lózia Beniére*, the *Lózia Chandakioû*, also known as the Lower Lózia, while the most northerly, which is smaller and of a rather different design, with steps running through it and an ancient pillar on one side supporting a couple of arches, is called Portáki.[2]

The castle, at the northern end of the town, is a battered shell, roughly rectangular, with an entrance on the west. There are the remains of a second storey, of arched embrasures, of internal dividing walls, but it is an amorphous clutter that offers little hint of departed glories, and might have been anything. Except for one relic. Built into a whitewashed wall, at a point that was perhaps the entrance to the castle enclosure, is a pillar on which is carved 'Da Koronia. 1365. MCCCLXV'. This was erected by Januli II da Corogna, who did a great deal of building at Kastron.

Next to the castle on the south is the old Latin church of St Antonio, with coloured Turkish plates embedded in its brickwork. Its entrance is now permanently blocked up, and one can get only a tantalizing glimpse of the interior through a breach, which was once a window, high on the north wall —a glimpse that just enables one to see dimly a vaulted roof. Close at hand is a house that has above the door the familiar Crispo lozenges, with I. C. and the date 1551; a little farther away a short length of classical wall looks very distinguished, with its beautifully squared stones, amid the medieval rubble masonry around. So, everywhere in Kastron the classical and romantic ages intermingle; if the heraldic shields, the gates, the bridges and the loopholed houses are much in evidence, one notices also the bases of ancient pillars in the street, marble capitals turned into doorsteps, and fragments of sculpture built into a wall.

Yet despite the walls and gates and tumbledown castle, Kastron holds no suggestion of blood and strife; even the pirates have left no memory to darken the aura of the place. It is the most peaceful town I know in the Cyclades, and wandering through the odd maze of streets at different levels, which looks as if it might have been designed by an ingenious child out of blocks on the nursery floor, one can hardly believe in its stormy past. It is shut in on itself without being on the defensive; its walls are no more martial than those of any row of houses, its arched gateways are merely cool and shady retreats for a siesta, its castle has fallen to ruin, because, one feels, there was never any need for it. One has reached the true Avilion 'crown'd with summer sea'—its only sentinel, posted on a point of land reaching into this sea, being the tiny church of the Seven Martyrs, holding up its cross to ban any intruder on the peace.

As we came away from Kastron, we saw in the valley to the west the two domed buildings known as the School of Siphnos, or the School of the Holy Tomb, which for two hundred years was famous throughout the Aegean, and included among its pupils many who were later eminent. The School appears to have come into being in 1653 at the Monastery of Chrysostomos, which lies not far away, but in 1687 it moved here. 'Nicholas Chrysogelos,' says Bent, 'was headmaster of this school at the time of the outbreak of the war of independence. He forthwith initiated his scholars into the mysteries of the Friendly Society, and when, on March 25, 1821, the banner of freedom was unfurled, Chrysogelos took those of his pupils who were fit to carry arms and joined the army in the Peloponnese.' [3]

In 1834, when its buildings were crumbling and its finances much depleted, the School returned to Chrysostomos, where it carried on for another twenty years. The site at the Holy Tomb is enclosed by a wall, and is now the cemetery of Kastron.[4]

The next morning we set out to contact Mr Troullos, the President of the local Tourist Committee, who was also the schoolmaster. We found him teaching in his school at Lower Petáli. It was a fine, airy classroom, with about fifty little boys and girls, sitting two at a desk, who eyed us with avid curiosity, and no little amusement, nearly suppressed—for they were beautifully behaved—but not quite. Around the walls were large crude pictures concerned with what is, for the modern Greek, the beginning of history, the War of Independence.

Here was Archbishop Germanos raising the standard at the Monastery of Ayia Lavra near Kalavryta; here was Marco Bozaris leading his men, presumably at the great fight at Karpenisi; and here of course, as large as the pictures in a communist march, were portraits of Kolokotronis, Miaoulis, Ypsilantis and all the rest.

It is always a shock to be faced with the assumption that Greece is a young nation, and one has to accustom oneself to it; but that is certainly, in my experience, the way Greeks prefer to regard it. It is understandable that they do not feel able to annex the glories of classical Greece to their heritage, even though they like to claim descent from the ancient Greeks; but it is odd that they do not appear to look back with pride, and as a matter of course, to Byzantium. Not even to those memorable achievements of its final period, when Greeks recaptured Constantinople, and later the Peloponnesus, from the Latins; and when the last Greek emperor, Constantine, put up his heroic fight to save Constantinople from the Turks —flinging himself in despair at the end, with only two companions at his side, upon the hosts of the enemy. I should have liked to have seen him on the wall here among the others.

Mr Troullos, who is the author of a most informative little book on Siphnos, was very helpful; we saw him again on several occasions, were taken round his private museum, and were indebted to him for many kindnesses. From his school, we went on to the Chrysostomos. Standing near by, on a low hill overlooking the sea, to the north-west of Kastron, it consists of a small whitewashed church, with a drum and dome, dating from about 1500, neighboured by the ruins of ancient monastic buildings. One of the cells has been restored, and another partially so, with a deep, arched window that frames a view of Kastron; in the courtyard, which is starred with yellow hawkweed and tiny wild delphiniums, there grows a single tall palm that has, leaning against its trunk, a stone, recently discovered, with the date 1653, the year of the founding here of the School of Siphnos. From this palm tree the monastery acquired the name of 'The Plantation'. (Plate XVI)

In 1671 the monastery was turned into a nunnery, and remained as such until it was abolished by the government of King Otho in 1834. It was then that the School moved back here from the Holy Tomb.

We found it a bewitching place that led us to echo Hume, who wrote to Madame de Boufflers: 'Might we not settle in some Greek island, and breathe the air of Homer, or Sappho, or Anacreon in tranquillity, and great opulence?' On the other hand, it would do equally well for a hermit, especially if he were a beginner and a little lacking in confidence. For it is solitary, without being either hemmed in or remote; it has a wide horizon, and the busy world is comfortingly at hand, not a stone's throw away, at Kastron and at Apollonia. Even on this very hot day there was a breeze here, inducing a sibilant murmur in the palm tree to add company to the solitude, and, with the mutter of the sea, to break that dead, faintly intimidating silence that overtakes the Greek world when the high and mighty sun is harrying the land. Moreover, it is a stimulating place, the effect of it is to alert the mind, and create in it a fancy that it is gleaning ultimate wisdom from that quiet interchange between the sea and the palm tree. And surely that is the only recipe for a happy hermit; for where indeed are the charms of solitude if it be merely a narcotic and not a tonic? Anyway, Chrysostomos is undoubtedly the ideal site for a school, and must have provided an enviable memory for Old Chrysostomosians!

We left it toward evening. Viewed from a little way off in the fading light, the palm tree, next the white dome of the church, stood up grotesquely in that bare landscape, ruffling its plumes like a gigantic, long-legged bird that had flown out of the Stymphalian bog, and was brooding over a monstrous egg.

Back in Apollonia, we made our way to the restaurant which was run by a cheerful, voluble, colourful, and kindly old lady who, with a bandana twisted rakishly round her head, looked more the type to tell your fortune than toss you up an omelette, but who in fact could not only boil an egg as admirably as Mr Woodhouse's Serle, but make the most delicious cakes—otherwise, well, our advice to those patronizing her restaurant would be 'Let them eat cake'!

On the day we were due to leave Siphnos, we were told at the hotel that the boat had been cancelled. We accepted this warily; but further inquiries showed that this time Rumour was speaking with a single tongue, and had it right. We used the extra day to take up a challenge that had been presenting itself to me ever since we arrived. To the west of Apollonia is the long ridge, about 2,000 feet high, of Mount Prophet Elias, and perched on the summit is the monastery of that name. Aileen could contemplate that white blob in the clouds with equanimity, but I have what might be called a beanstalk complex, an illogical conviction that if only one climbs, one will arrive at the strange and wonderful! I have the greatest urge to get to the top. Aileen agreed reluctantly to make the ascent to the monastery—as she always does on these occasions, aware that at least there will be a view—and we started off.

It proved a much easier climb than we had expected. The path rounds the south flank of the ridge, and winds up from the west, and we reached the monastery after two and a half hours. It was quite deserted. Like the monastery on Seriphos, it consisted of a rectangular defensive enclosure with a church in the centre. There is a tradition that it was founded by the Empress Irene in the eighth century, but the church, although recently rebuilt, had probably been put up originally in 1686, the date over its door. It had a very odd, piebald appearance, its grey stone being mottled with leprous patches of a white cement-like material; the effect was that of a clumsy attempt at camouflage, and indeed it may be akin to that. For the monastery has always been a target for the thunderbolts of a jealous Zeus, and again and again it has been struck: twenty years ago it was badly damaged, ten years later it was almost completely destroyed, and it was then rebuilt, so we were told, with a material that is less attractive to lightning. Hence, perhaps, the peculiar masonry.

On the south of the enclosure, beneath a row of cells, was a passage giving access to underground rooms, where the monastery's treasures were hidden when pirates were raiding. Incidentally, one of the worst raids experienced here was in the year 1609 by English pirates, who were only driven off when a Turkish fleet arrived unexpectedly.

We sat there for long on the shady side of the courtyard, enjoying the quiet; until suddenly out of the blue overhead came a raucous croak, and looking up, we saw two ravens hovering.

Towards six o'clock that evening we went down to the village square with our rucksacks to catch the bus to Kamares. As we drew near, we were startled by a wild, melancholy cry that rose from it—a cry that, to borrow Miranda's phrase, did knock against the very heart. We hurried forward nervously, prepared for drama—to find it was the fishmonger. Surrounded by his baskets of fish, he invited trade by uttering in a long, high-pitched wail the one word: 'Psar-i-a!!'

The bus was long in coming, and eventually we accepted an offer from the local taxi to take us down to Kamares at the bargain price of sixteen drachmae. At Kamares, we sat in a café, ordered coffee, and began the routine vigil. It was 6.45. The only other occupant was the woman in charge, who was knitting placidly. We were tired and not inclined to talk; the light was too bad to read; and we waited for the siren, slumped on our hard chairs, in nearly as much discomfort as Odysseus bound to his mast. Overcome with boredom, I looked round for any object of interest. In addition to the inevitable glass-sided counter, there was a long shelf of bottles, which gave the barn-like room an unexpectedly professional air, but the effect was marred by two cabinets packed with ornamental china, more appropriate to the front parlour than the saloon bar. The walls were something of a compromise: there were two foxes' heads carved in wood, and next them, as if to contrast art and nature, two dead crayfish; there were family photographs of people with that defiant glare characteristic of those who have never before confronted a camera, and are unhappily aware that this is the moment of truth; there was a dashing poster advertising 'Golden Years with the People's Lottery', and next to it, no doubt as a sample of what those golden years might hold, a crude print of two Spanish girls, and another of a bullfight. I continued to be bored: why is there never a pin-table, or a dartboard, or even a picture book in these quayside cafés, which, to the impatient traveller, are a kind of purgatory between time and eternity, where the one has definitely stopped and the other appears to have begun, and appals one with its emptiness! It would seem that the Mediterranean genius is indeed, in Buffon's phrase, an aptitude for patience. Heaven be praised, however, that one of the things the cafés lack is a juke-box.

At the end of an hour and a half the café began to fill, and the ticket agent arrived: we devoutly hoped he was a dove who betokened the approach of the ark. We passed another three-quarters of an hour hoping. No-one, evidently, was there for a jolly evening and a spot of beer, they were all waiting for the boat, and in no time they were as bored and apathetic as we were, until someone brought in a small boy—who I now realized was the more economical equivalent of a pin-table, for there is always a small boy.

Animation had practically become suspended in us, when the bray came, and brought us to life again as joyously as saints at the Last Trump.

Yet I have a pleasant memory of Kamares, for when the boat arrived, there was none of the usual devil-take-the-hindmost procedure: we were relieved of our rucksacks, and escorted to a rowboat, nor did we see our baggage again until we were aboard the ship. Nobody appeared to expect a tip, but I was delighted to give them one, for this was more than kindness, this was service!

Chapter Twelve

MELOS

Pirate Entrepôt

THE ship was the old *Limnos*, which we hadn't encountered since leaving Naxos. We spent two hours sitting comfortably in her second-class lounge, and it was getting on for midnight when we reached Adamas, the port of Melos. We walked down the gangway on to the quay, where quite a crowd had gathered—and at once we were 'shanghaied' in the most polite way imaginable!

We knew there was a good hotel at Adamas, the Poseidon, and we had decided to go there, so when a woman approached, and offered me rooms, I shook my head, and said: 'The Poseidon.'

'It is full,' she replied.

I was frankly sceptical. It was late in the season, many hotels were closed, and it was unlikely that one would be full. So I insisted firmly that I was going to the Poseidon. A policeman pointed out the direction, and we marched off—but the woman was not to be eluded, and followed, protesting again that the hotel was full. Somewhat embarrassed by having to exhibit my disbelief, but determined to try the Poseidon, I walked on, smiling at her as benevolently as I could manage. We arrived at the Poseidon, to find it in complete darkness; I pushed open the door, and called out. There was no answer. Plainly they were not expecting any arrivals from the boat, and it looked as if the woman were right.

At this moment a man came up to me, and assured me the

hotel was full. Reluctantly accepting this, I asked to be directed to the other hotel, the Aphrodite.

'Ah! The Aphrodite!' exclaimed the woman. 'I will show you.'

Still more embarrassed, I followed her, and she brought us to the side entrance of a house on the quay.

'The Aphrodite?' I inquired doubtfully.

'Yes, yes, the Aphrodite,' she replied.

I was quite sure it was not, and murmured as much to Aileen; but by this time my nerve was broken. I could not, after being proved wrong once, go on plainly indicating that I thought she was a liar. It was a reasonable looking place; so we decided to take a chance on it.

It was not of course the Aphrodite. As we immediately discovered, it was the private house of an elderly widow, a relative of the woman who had captured us. Letting rooms was the widow's only source of income, and as often as a boat came in, all her family formed themselves into a press-gang, and went down to the quay to gather in new arrivals. I felt I was more or less quits now with our captor, and I could excuse her desperate effort on her relative's behalf; but I must admit I was a trifle taken aback when, a day or two later, we were invited to her house, and, rocking with laughter at the sight of me, she exclaimed: 'Ha! ha! You thought it was the Aphrodite!'

Our landlady, who had been a widow for thirty-five years, was something of a charmer, and her house was clean and well kept; but our bedroom was a daunting affair resembling a Victorian lumber-room. It was not so large, but deployed along one wall was a formidable sideboard with platoons of cupboards and a long rank of drawers; against another wall a great hall-stand reared up to the ceiling with hat-pegs sprouting from it everywhere that at night, when the moon shone through the window, gleamed like the stalked eyes of a rampant Argus; and there was a large circular table, inlaid and polished, that would not have seemed undignified at

Camelot. Among all this furniture we sidled and edged, depositing a couple of handkerchiefs in a drawer that would have held all the robes in Priam's treasury, or draping underclothes on Argus, where they hung like rags on a skeleton.

The family gang did all they could to make us comfortable; but the beds were as hard as mortuary slabs, the quay noisy, and at five in the morning—and every morning afterwards—we were woken by the fishermen going to work in their outboard-motorboats.

Adamas has quite an imposing front for an island port, with a broad, curving sweep of quay, upstanding buildings, and a view over one of the finest harbours in the Mediterranean. As in the case of Santorin, this is the crater of a volcano, though here the volcano is extinct, and it forms almost a complete oval. Opposite Adamas, on the perimeter, is the mountain called, inevitably, Prophet Elias; while a little to the north of the town is the gap in the crater, about a mile wide, that provides the entrance to the harbour.

After an excellent breakfast—at the Poseidon, where they confirmed that the hotel was indeed full, owing to the presence of engineers working on a new jetty—we caught a bus to Plakes, one of the four villages that are scattered round the conical hill, a mile or so to the north, on which the Venetian castle was built.

Melos played its part in affairs long before the classical period, for the ruins at Phylakopí, the obsidian city on the north coast, are older than Homeric Troy, and go back to the Early Bronze Age, to about 3000 B.C. The classical city was at Klima, below Plakes on the eastern side of the harbour entrance, and here was enacted in 416 B.C. the tragedy described in the fifth book of Thucydides, when the Athenians blotted out the city.

Under the Dukes, Melos would appear to have remained a personal appanage of the Sanudi and Crispi, and was usually held by a member of the ruling family. Towards the end of the thirteenth century there was a rebellion on the island, and, led by a Greek monk, the rebels captured the castle; but the Duke, Marco II, that no-nonsense ruler who had dealt so drastically with 'Saint Fat' on Naxos, descended on the island like a thunderbolt. Aided by a few French adventurers from Constantinople, he retook the castle in two hours, and made an example of the monk by binding him hand and foot, and flinging him into the sea. Apart from this cruelty, however, the medieval conqueror was more humane than the classical, for he spared all the monk's followers.

In the following century Melos had its share of the normal Aegean miseries, being sacked by the Catalans, and captured by the Genoese, but the Sanudi managed nevertheless to recover it. In 1383 the ruler of Melos was Francesco Crispo, who had obtained the island through his wife, and who in that year murdered the last Sanudo Duke, and stepped into his shoes. Thereafter Melos's fortunes were those of the rest of the Duchy: it was subject on different occasions to Venetian rule, and fell with the other islands to the Turks in 1566.

During the Turkish dominion it enjoyed considerable notoriety as the headquarters of piracy in the Aegean, as a kind of pirate entrepôt where the loot was auctioned off. One of these pirates, the Provençal, Hugues Creveliers, Byron's 'Corsair', who has been mentioned in connection with his raid on Andros, had a reputation for being more humane than his brethren; another, a Greek, Joannes Kopsi, actually seized Melos in 1677, but three years later he was decoyed aboard a Turkish vessel, and executed. The Melians found this plague of pirates an unbearable infliction, and a number of them, under the leadership of their Archbishop, together with a few Samians, emigrated to London in the days of Charles II. 'It is to this colony that Greek Street owes its name, for the Duke of York, the future King James II, assigned that site to them as a residence, and in Hog Lane, afterwards called Crown Street, Soho, they built a Greek church—the first in London.' [1]

We walked from Plakes up to the castle, and found it disappointing. Here again it seems that two lines of fortifications once circled the hill, except on the steep eastern face, but they are barely traceable. The remaining walls, some of which are only two or three feet high, have been tidied up with cement, and occasionally topped with a hideous kind of grey brick grid, so that they no longer retain a medieval air, but look as though they belonged to a barracks or a prison. Only toward the north are there parts of the old curtain that have been allowed to crumble in an undisciplined but not unsatisfying way, with a narrow, truly medieval lane winding up through them to recall the past. (Plate XVII)

There is, however, one delightful relic not far below the summit on the west, the little chapel of Duke Giovanni IV, which forms what is practically an additional aisle to the later church of Panayia Thalassi, Our Lady of the Sea. The chapel has its own entrance on the west, and above this are the Crispo lozenges, with I. C. and the date 1552—the arms of Giovanni IV, son of the mad Duke, who escaped the murderous attack by his father, and became the last but one of the Latin Dukes of the Archipelago. Entering the chapel, one finds it a narrow rectangle with a flat roof, three square embrasure-like windows on the south, and opposite them, giving access to the church, three low, pointed arches, with a fourth beyond the templon, or reredos. Nothing could be simpler, but it is a wonderfully forceful simplicity that has built to the glory of God in a confident humility scornful of bedizenment; and to wander from it into its large, and more ornate, neighbour is inevitably to feel the latter vulgar.

From the castro one has a good view, to the west, of the harbour entrance, and of the little hill near Klima that was once the acropolis of the classical town. The vale of Klima is as lovely and peaceful a setting for a massacre as I have ever met: a long terrace lodged among the hills, fenced in by them to the north and east, but dropping abruptly to the harbour entrance on the south, it is cradled between hills and the sea, and blessed by both, sheltered yet airy, with the movement and sparkle of the water to break its somnolence. Coming from

Trypiti, one sees in front the knoll, crowned with a chapel, on which was one of the two acropolises, and beneath which is the site of the Greek theatre. On the right of the road are lengths of wall that mark the east gate of the city, and on the left is the steep declivity, near the top of which was found, in 1820, the statue of the Venus de Milo. (Plate XVIII)

At the foot of the slope is a Roman theatre with eight of its tiers of marble seats; nearby is a stretch of ancient wall built of squared blocks of volcanic rock that are a magnificent royal purple, so that in the setting sun the wall glows as though it were the battlement of a legend, built of precious stones. Not far away, to the east, tunnelled into the tufa rock of the hillside, are Christian catacombs. We were shown over these by the curator of the little museum in Plakes. They are finely arranged: the low galleries are lit by tiny electric bulbs fitted into replicas of Roman lamps, one on each tomb, pinpoints of light that shine in an endless chain through the pitch blackness like an image of the Christian faithful in a pagan world.

Next morning we took a bus to Zephyria, the old medieval capital, which lies on the south-east of the island, and which, because malaria was so prevalent there, was gradually deserted by its inhabitants, and was finally abandoned in the middle of the nineteenth century by the last fever-stricken wrecks who had clung to it. Today, a small modern village is grouped about the old church, which has the date 1645 over its main door; while the relics of the ancient city lie in the surrounding fields and olive groves—long piles of stones, banked on either side of what were once the streets, and stretching on through the trees and grass. It is a scene that induces an uncomfortable, even eerie feeling; for the strange thing is that nowhere along these lines of debris is there a single fragment of wall standing, and one has a vision of a goaded and terrified people tearing down the accursed city, determined not to let one stone remain in place on another. We saw no-one there. Only a donkey, entirely on its own, stepped delicately down one of the ghostly streets, and might have been the representative of some Houyhnhnm civilization that had succeeded the vanished world of men. (Plate XIX)

On our third and last day, we took a taxi out to Phylakopí, some five or six miles away, on the north coast. It is on a wild and windy shore, where the volcanic cliff confronts the blue water with a grey face, and grapples it with bony arms that end in livid fingers and knuckles of rock that are barely awash. For it is a soft rock, and in places the sea has eaten far into it, and can be heard gurgling and gulping all about one. This is no exaggeration, for as we stood on the cliff facing the sea, Aileen said to me: 'I can hear water behind us!'

I thought she must be mistaken, but when we turned inland from this point, which we had approached along the coast, we found our way barred by a narrow inlet, fifty or sixty yards in length, where the sea had tunnelled through the cliff, and was carrying out a great encircling movement.

The ancient city, excavated by the British in 1896–9, and again in 1910–11, owed its importance to the fact that it abounded in obsidian, the black volcanic glass that, before the discovery of metal, was invaluable for spearheads and cutting blades; many fragments of this are still to be found, and we picked up a handful in a few minutes. The site is now a jumble of stones that has nothing to tell the inexpert eye, except that along the top of the cliff, parallel to the sea, is a stretch of archaic wall. This is a relic of the third city, which faded out in the late twelfth century B.C. after the Dorian invasion of the mainland, and the general collapse of the Mycenaean world.

We walked on four or five kilometres to Pollonia, the little village opposite the island of Kimolos, which is divided from Melos by a strip of water only a little over half a mile wide. As we stood waiting near the quayside for our bus, we watched a couple of men who were apparently digging foundations for a house. Suddenly one of them gave an exclamation, and stooping down, picked up a skull. He and his companion examined it, and then, digging around, unearthed a number of other human bones.

A few schoolchildren gathered to eye the finds with interest, but the men were merely amused, and as unconcerned as the grave-digger in Hamlet, and one couldn't help wondering if with them, too, 'Custom hath made it . . . a property of easiness'. For in these islands where there has been such continual violence through the ages, and where many and many a corpse must have been interred in hugger-mugger, skeletons probably crop up with some frequency.

Chapter Thirteen

PAROS

The Guns of Bernard Sagredo

THAT night, for once, we did not have to wait for the boat in the desolation of a café, but sat in state in our landlady's house—surrounded by the 'press gang' who were fully mobilized for the occasion. Our boat, the *Despina*, arrived at nine; we were travelling first, and this time our cabin was habitable, if not particularly comfortable, with a porthole that opened.

All the same, we didn't manage to get much sleep, and it was a rather wan-looking couple that trailed reluctantly on to the quay at the Piraeus at seven in the morning. At this hour the Piraeus is at its worst; in the pale, early morning light, it, too, has a haggard look, an abandoned, moribund air as if it were but another relic in this land of relics, though from a more recent past. We shouldered our rucksacks, plodded to the metro, caught a train to Monasterion station, and so to our hotel in the Plaka.

Soon after midday we were afloat again, in the *Pandelis*, bound for Paros, where we arrived at 10 p.m. We were at once aware that this was a more sophisticated island: the boat tied up to the quay, a porter carried our rucksacks on a wheelbarrow to our hotel, the hotel was not only clean, but had really comfortable beds, adequate plumbing, and even a respectable lavatory. There was of course no hot water—but in the Aegean hot water comes out of a tap as rarely as, elsewhere, it comes out of the earth. Moreover, next day, we found a restaurant

175

that had some idea of cooking and serving: the first we had come across, outside Athens, since we had left Syra.

After breakfast at our hotel, we explored the little town, and the remains of the castle. Paroikia is laid out with one long, narrow main street that is always a delightful place in which to idle—shady in the heat, protected from the wind on cold days, pleasantly decked at intervals with balconies hung with bougainvillaea, and offering for distraction a leisurely, soothing activity.

In classical times Paros was celebrated for its marble, and as the birthplace of Archilocus, that bitter, cynical, disillusioned 'old sweat', who happened also to be a great poet. Something of the island's history from the coming of the Venetians has already been told, for this was the island that Maria Sanudo, daughter of Spezzabanda, was given by Francesco I Crispo in 1483, on condition that she gave up Andros and married Gasparo di Sommaripa; and here the Sommaripa ruled, with many ups and downs, which included, in 1503, a war between the Paros and Andros members of the family, until, in 1517, the male line became extinct.

In 1537 the island was owned by Cecilia Venier, who was married to Bernard Sagredo, and in that year Barbarossa fell upon it. He was met by a gallant resistance from Sagredo, whose defence was almost the last noteworthy feat of arms performed by the Franks before the Duchy of the Archipelago came to an end.

Sagredo, with a Florentine outlaw as an ally, had only a handful of fighting men, and he was forced to yield the castle at Naoussa, but, shutting himself in Ayios Antonios, he made a number of effective sorties, and held Barbarossa at bay. But eventually his powder ran out, and he was compelled to surrender. Six thousand of the inhabitants were thereupon subjected to Barbarossa's routine retaliation of massacre, slavery or rape, while the boys were enrolled in the corps of janissaries. But Miller tells us that Cecilia 'was allowed to withdraw to Venice, and Sagredo himself was soon released from captivity, thanks to the gratitude of a Ragusan sailor who had once rowed in a galley under his command'.[1]

After that, except for a short period just before the end of the Duchy, when the island was returned by the Sultan to the Duke, Paros remained in Turkish hands.

In common with the rest of the Archipelago, it was constantly plagued by the corsairs. It made no difference if some of them were technically privateers carrying letters of marque, for they behaved as pirates, and took what they wanted anywhere they could find it. One of the main reasons for their forays was the demand for, and value of, slaves to row in the galleys, which remained for long the normal warships of the Mediterranean. The slave trade was a very flourishing business indeed; nor were the Christians at all behind the Musselmen in their pursuit of it: 'At Pisa, at Marseilles, at Genoa, at Livorno and elsewhere, actual companies fitted out for the harvest of human flesh in the Aegean, and sold their merchandise in the special market at Livorno.'[2] So dreadful were the memories of one man who had served aboard a corsair on these slave raids that he declared he would rather 'be a slave for seven years in Algiers than live sixteen months on a corsair'.[3]

It was during these years of Ottoman rule that the family of Mavroyéni, closely connected with Paros and Mykonos, rose to eminence among those Greeks who served the Ottoman Empire in many high offices, and who were known, from Phanari, the quarter in Constantinople in which they dwelt and in which the Greek Patriarch had his seat, as Phanariots. To this family belonged Mandô Mavroyéni, whom we have seen in the War of Independence commanding a company of palikaris under Odysseus at the battle near Kárystos. She fought on other fronts in Greece with her company, but her services were ill-rewarded, and eventually, in 1840, having given all she possessed to the cause of independence, she died in poverty here at Paros.

The castle at Paroikia stands in the town on a slight eminence that was the ancient acropolis. Reputedly built by Marco I Sanudo, it exhibits now only a single ruined tower with a short length of wall, but it is all the same an odd and unforgettable relic. For the tower was built from material quarried out of classical buildings, and great blocks of marble alternate with drums from the shafts of columns, laid end on, and forming in one place a row of eight solid discs that gives the appearance of a storey on a rolling bogey. (Plate XX) There the interest ends, for the ruin is a mere façade, the interior being occupied by modern houses built against the old wall that is crowned with whitewashed battlements.

We were naturally very anxious to see the castle of Ayios Antonios, where Sagredo had made his last stand, more particularly as Scott O'Connor, in his *Isles of the Aegean*, had said that the guns used by Sagredo and many cannon balls from the siege were still to be seen in the courtyard of the chapel. So at 7.45 the next morning we caught a bus to Márpissa, which is an ancient village, built up a slope, with narrow lanes, many archways, here and there a coat of arms, and among the churches one that bears the date 1423. Just to the north of the village is Ayios Antonios, on a conical hill that rises 750 feet above the little bay of Marmara—a favourite lurking place of Creveliers, the pirate.

The castle, also known as Kephalos from the northern headland of the bay, was built in the late fifteenth century by Niccolò Sommaripa, but has now almost gone. Apart from the church on the summit, nothing remains except a few lengths of wall, a ruined bastion or two, several barrel-roofed buildings in various stages of decay, two of which were probably chapels, and any amount of debris.

The only interesting feature is the church, attached to which are some rooms that once formed part of a tiny monastery. In front of the west door is an attractive little paved court, bounded on the north by an arched passage. Into this we stepped eagerly: it was the place described by O'Connor. There was a rubber tree and a myrtle, and a well with a marble surround bearing what might be a classical carving—but there were neither guns nor cannon balls.

Could they, we wondered, conceivably be inside the church? We tried the door. It was locked. So were the doors to the monastic rooms. We peered through keyholes, and small windows, but could see nothing. It was a great disappointment —they would, I thought, have been evocative relics in a place where so little was left to bring before the mind's eye that last stand, and what the local guidebook describes as the 'fierceful' attacks of Barbarossa.

In Márpissa, waiting for the bus, I questioned everyone in the café. No-one, quite plainly, had ever heard of Bernard Sagredo, and my constant repetition of the word *purobólon*, 'cannon', mystified them utterly. They looked upon me with awe: it was true, then, that all Englishmen were mad. I gave it up—until we got back to Paroikia. Then I started again. I was obstinately determined; somewhere, somehow, I would run to earth these vile guns.

I dragged Aileen round to the small classical museum, found a young man who spoke French, and poured out my story. But either my French, or the mysterious syllables 'Sagredo' worked on him like an incantation: his wits left him, he could only goggle, and dazed, lead me to the curator in his office. I bombarded the curator with my *purobólon*. He knew nothing, and was inclined to be suspicious. Who was I? What did I want this information for? I explained impatiently I was writing a book on Greek castles. That was fatal. He wanted to know everything I had written, with titles! But, eventually, I wore him down, and got away with a single fact: abutting on the courtyard of the church of the Hundred Gates were rooms given over to a Byzantine museum, and this had a guardian. Possibly he might be able to help me—though it was evident the curator thought a psychiatrist would do better.

We hurried round to the Hundred Gates, but the guardian was out, taking part in a service in the church, and reluctantly, I abandoned the quest for the moment. In conversation with an acquaintance, a retired British naval officer who was living on Paros, I learnt that among the monks at a nearby monastery was an Englishman who, said my companion, was an Oxford man and extremely well-informed, and it was suggested that I might apply to him. But I gathered he was not anxious to make contact with the outside world, and my nerve failed me at the idea of intruding upon the recluse's meditations with a trifling and perhaps obnoxious query concerning carnal weapons!

Next morning I tackled the guardian, after tactfully paying a visit to his museum. It seemed that the name of Sagredo did rouse some echo in his mind, and finally he gave it as his opinion that the guns were inside the church of Ayios Antonios. It was probably a guess, but it was enough! I rushed Aileen to the square; we hired a taxi; and drove to Márpissa for the second time.

There, an elderly lady guided us to the *papas*, who had the keys of the church. She, herself, appeared overcome at meeting an English couple, and as she led us through the streets, chattering volubly and incomprehensibly, she would pause now and then to look at us, and to murmur in wonder: '*Agglos! Agglos!*' ('English! English!').

The *papas* was cementing the floor of one of his churches, but he kindly sent someone for the keys. Clutching these, we set off up the hill again. But, alas, when we opened the church, there were no guns. The little place was worth a visit, with its dim frescoes, and, on the floor, a fine double-headed eagle, and two coats of arms marking tombs; but I was disappointed, and gave it but a cursory glance. We were able to open the doors of the monastic rooms, but had no better luck there.

It was the *papas*, however, who offered the most reasonable solution, when, on returning the keys, I mentioned Sagredo. He said he thought the guns had disappeared during the German occupation of Paros in the war. No doubt the metal made them worth looting.

On the way back we visited Drio, just south of Márpissa, where the Capitan Pasha used to anchor his fleet when he came to collect the tribute from the islands. A place of evil memories for Greeks, it is today a depressing village, with a flat foreshore, and a long, low island in the offing that has a reptilian look, as though it were the coil of a basking sea-serpent.

We had determined to leave Paros that night, but back at Paroikia we were told that the sailing had been cancelled. Nor, as usual, was there any unanimity on whether there would be a boat next day. But on the following morning, opinion had hardened; it was generally held there would be a sailing, and one agent was willing to back his judgment to the extent of issuing us tickets.

His name was Krispi, and I felt sure he must be a descendant of the ducal Crispi—displaying all the venturesome initiative of his race! I mentioned this conjecture to a Greek who was staying in our hotel, and he confirmed that this was quite probably the case. There were, he added, still Sanudi in Naxos, and Gozzadini in Athens.

We spent the day loitering in Paroikia, but I only retain a vivid memory of one small scene—a private school of music, where one adult pupil was practising with laborious determination on an accordion. It was a small room on the ground floor with a door giving directly on the street: the door was open, and he sat there all alone, going over and over a single phrase, enraptured by his virtuosity and utterly oblivious of the world beyond the door, and the two aliens who contemplated him with such unashamed interest—or if he noticed, he no doubt assumed that we, too, were entranced by his performance. But in fact we were held simply by a picture of innocent and unalloyed happiness. On the door was a notice offering to teach the accordion, the guitar, the melodion, or singing, for 100 drachmae a month, which we thought very reasonable as a fee for tuition, and even more reasonable as a fare to Paradise!

We were at the quay with our rucksacks at 6.30, and were taken aback at the scene; nowhere else in all our journeying among the islands, not even at Naxos or Syra, had we encountered such a company waiting for the boat. The big café on the quay was packed to bursting, opaque with tobacco smoke, and clamorous with talk: it was plain that Paros was a thriving centre of affairs.

It was two hours before the boat came, and we all stampeded for the narrow jetty that runs out from the quay—only to find the way barred by sailors.

It appeared that the ship, the 'fast *Karaiskakês*', being deeper in draught than her companions, had to keep about fifty yards from the jetty, while a ferry service was run over this short distance for the passengers.

The delay continued a long time, and the crowd grew restive. Some in it had had a stirrup-cup or two, and a violent altercation broke out between those ahead and the sailors. There were shouts and oaths, the whole body of us shuddered and swayed to and fro as those behind cried 'Forward!', and those in front cried whatever abusive word occurred to them, as the sailors thrust them back; arms rose threateningly against the starlit sky, and a fight seemed inevitable. But in Greece one must never judge the seriousness of the situation by the noise; presently exhaustion set in, voices died down, and people relaxed after a stimulating row. At which point our acquaintance of the hotel stepped forward, and spoke a few words to the sailors. He seemed a person of some authority; at any rate they made way for us, and, somewhat self-consciously, we disengaged ourselves from the hoi polloi, and stepped on to the jetty.

This last trip was notable in another way. We had travelled on the *Karaiskakês* before, but never in the first class; and now we found ourselves, for the one and only time in our Aegean wanderings, wallowing in luxury. We had dinner on board, and it was impeccable, not even Aladdin's genie could have done better; our cabin had every possible comfort, and the plumbing worked as smoothly as if it had been in the Ritz. Next morning we should be turning our backs sadly on the Aegean, this eternally beguiling realm of silver-footed Thetis, but assuredly the gods had exerted themselves to bring us home on our last voyage, as they brought Odysseus home to Ithaca, loaded with gifts.

Table of Events

1263	About this date Philanthropenos, admiral of the Greek Emperor Michael VIII, attacks the islands. Shortly afterwards Melos rises in revolt, but is quickly crushed by the third Duke of Naxos, Marco II Sanudo.
1275	Battles of Neopatras and Demetrias.
1275 to 1285	Most of Euboea, and many of the islands are reconquered for the Greeks by Licario, the Italian renegade.
1286	War of the Ass between Marco II's son, Guglielmo of Syra, and one of the Ghisi of Mykonos.
1292	The Aragonese admiral, Roger de Lluria, ravages Andros, Mykonos, Tenos and Kythnos.
1294	Bonifacio da Verona marries Agnes de Cicon, the dispossessed heiress of Castel Rosso.
1296 to 1303	War between Venice and Greek Empire. Most of the islands taken by Licario are regained by the Latins.
1296	Bonifacio da Verona recaptures Castel Rosso and Larmena.
1307	Siphnos seized by Januli da Corogna, who declares himself an independent sovereign. Januli Gozzadini does the same at Anaphê.
1309	Knights of St John capture Rhodes from Turkish corsairs. They also occupy Delos.
1310	Greek rule has now been eliminated from the islands.
1311	Battle of Kephissos. Catalans occupy Athens.
1336	The Duchy at this time holds Naxos, Andros, Paros, Antiparos, Ios, Melos, Kimolos, Santorin, Syra. Kythnos, held by the Gozzadini, and Amorgos, under the Schiavi and Grimani, are vassals of the Duchy. But Venice has become the suzerain of Tenos and Mykonos, where the Ghisi rule; of Astypalaia, owned by the Quirini and Grimani; of Kea, divided between the Premarini and

Giustiniani; and of Seriphos, held by the Bragadini and Michieli.

1344   The Turks, led by a Genoese pirate, occupy lower town of Naxos, plunder island, and carry off 6,000 people.

1346   The Black Death.

1350   Venetian-Genoese war. Duke Giovanni I is taken
to   prisoner to Genoa. He is restored to his islands at
1355   the peace of 1355.

1361   Duke Giovanni I dies, and his daughter, Fiorenza, becomes Duchess of the Archipelago. She is kidnapped by Venice, and forced into a second marriage, with her cousin, Niccolò Sanudo (Spezzabanda), who acts as Duke.

1371   Fiorenza dies, and her son by her first husband becomes Duke, as Niccolò III.

1383   Niccolò III is murdered at Naxos by Francesco Crispo of Melos, who usurps the Dukedom, and founds a dynasty of the Crispi.
         Maria Sanudo marries Gasparo di Sommaripa, and they receive Paros.

1388   The Catalan Duchy of Athens falls to the Florentine Nerio Acciajuoli.

1390   The Ghisi die out. Tenos, Mykonos and Delos go to Venice.

1393   Adoldo's outrage at Seriphos.

1416   The Turks raid the Cyclades. Between the Turks and the pirates, some islands are almost depopulated.

1426   Venice being unable to help him, Giovanni II makes his own peace with the Turks, and is compelled to pay tribute.

1431   Venice ravages Genoese colony of Chios, and Genoa retaliates by seizing Naxos and Andros, but they are returned.

1440   Crusino I Sommaripa, Maria Sanudo's son, and lord of Paros, receives Andros.

1447   Gian Giacomo, a minor, succeeds to the Dukedom;
his grandmother, the dowager Duchess Francesca,
widow of Giovanni II, claims the regency, but is
imprisoned.

1452   Gian Giacomo dies, and in 1453 is succeeded by his
great-uncle, Guglielmo of Anaphê, as Guglielmo II.

1453   Constantinople taken by the Turks. During Guglielmo's reign (1453–63) the Turks also overthrow
the Greek Despotate of the Morea and the Florentine
Duchy of Athens.

1463   Venetian-Turkish war.
to   In 1470 Negroponte on Euboea is taken by the
1479   Turks.

1494   Duke Giovanni III dies, leaving only an illegitimate
son and daughter. In consequence the Duchy goes
to Venice. Venice now owns Naxos, Santorin, Syra,
Ios, Melos, Tenos, Mykonos and the northern
Sporades. Andros and Paros are held by the Sommaripa; Amorgos and Astypalaia by the Quirini;
Seriphos by the Michieli; Antiparos by the Loredani;
Siphnos, Kythnos and part of Kea by the Gozzadini;
the other part of Kea by the Premarini; and Anaphê
by Fiorenza Crispo.

1499   Venetian-Turkish war.
to   In 1500 Venice hands over Duchy to Francesco III,
1503   the illegitimate son of Giovanni III.
Naxos is twice attacked by the Turks, and the lower
town is taken and sacked.

1503   War between Sommaripa of Paros and Sommaripa
of Andros.

1510   Francesco III turns out to be a homicidal maniac,
and murders his wife.

1511   Venice takes over Duchy once more.

1517   Giovanni, son of the mad Duke, becomes Duke as
Giovanni IV. He is carried off by Turkish corsairs,
but Venice quickly ransoms him.

1522	Turks take Rhodes from Knights of St John.
1537	Venetian-Turkish war.
to	In 1537 the Turkish admiral, Khaireddin Barbarossa,
1540	descends upon the islands. Seriphos, Ios, Anaphê, Antiparos, Astypalaia, Mykonos and Amorgos are all taken. Paros also falls, after a gallant defence by Bernard Sagredo.
1537	Giovanni IV, at Naxos, surrenders to the Turks, and agrees to pay an annual tribute of 5,000 ducats. Nevertheless Naxos is plundered.
1538	Second cruise of Barbarossa. Skyros and Skiathos fall.
1540	Peace made. Tenos only Venetian possession left.
1566	The last Christian Duke, Giacomo IV, is imprisoned at Constantinople, and the Latin Duchy comes to an end. Joseph Nasi, a Jew, the favourite of the Sultan, becomes Duke. The Sommaripa are removed from Andros, and the Gozzadini from Siphnos.
1570	Venetian-Turkish war.
to	
1573	
1571	Cyprus taken by the Turks. Battle of Lepanto. Giacomo IV temporarily restored to his Duchy. The Gozzadini recover Siphnos.
1572	Turks retake Naxos.
1579	Nasi goes. Islands annexed to Turkish Empire. But the Gozzadini remain, as Turkish tributaries, holding Siphnos, Kythnos, Kimolos, Polinos, Pholegandros, Gyaros and Sikinos.
1617	The Gozzadini are finally dispossessed by the Turks.
1715	Tenos, held by Venice, the last remaining Latin possession in the Aegean, is surrendered to the Turks.
1821	Outbreak of War of Independence.

Notes

CHAPTER ONE

1 *Conversations of Lord Byron* by Thomas Medwin (1824), pp. 9–10
2 *Ellen Terry and Bernard Shaw: A Correspondence* (1931), p. 365
3 *Pausanias and Other Greek Sketches* by J. G. Frazer (London 1900), VIII, Phyle
4 *Odyssey* (Loeb trans. by A. T. Murray, 1953–60), VII, 321–2
5 Quoted in *Castles of the Morea* by Kevin Andrews (Princeton 1953), p. 185
6 *The Latins in the Levant* by William Miller (London 1908), pp. 470–7
7 *Sketches of a Yachting Cruise* by Major Gambier Parry (London 1889), ch. 8
8 See *Passport to Greece* by Leslie Finer (London 1964) for an account of the pistachio man, pp. 76–8

CHAPTER TWO

1 See *The History of Greece under Othoman and Venetian Dominion* by George Finlay (1856), pp. 227–8
2 *The Four Georges: George I* by W. M. Thackeray (1860)
3 *Impressions of Greece* by the Rt Hon. Sir Thomas Wyse, K.C.B., with an introduction by his niece, Miss Wyse (1871), p. 208
4 *Ibid*, p. 36

5　For a description of Licario, see *Dans les îles grecques avec les barons francs* by Michelle Avéroff (Paris 1963), p. 35
6　The Latins in the Levant, p. 577
7　In *Argolis* by George Horton (Chicago 1902), xxxviii
8　The Cyclades, or Life Among the Insular Greeks by J. Theodore Bent (London 1885), ch. XIII, p. 328
9　L'Empire Latin de Constantinople by Jean Longnon (Paris 1949), p. 244
10　Travels in Various Countries of the East ed. by the Rev. Robert Walpole, M.A. (London 1820), VI, pp. 72–3

CHAPTER THREE

1　Records of Shelley, Byron and the Author by Edward John Trelawny, ch. XX
2　Odyssey, III, 178–9
3　The Chronicle of Muntaner trans. from the Catalan by Lady Goodenough. Hakluyt Society, 2nd series, Nos. 47 (1920) and 50 (1921), Ch. CCXLIV
4　Ibid, ch. CCXL
5　Ibid, ch. CCXLIII
6　History of the Greek Revolution by George Finlay (1861), vol. II, pp. 8–9

CHAPTER FOUR

1　Travels in Various Countries of the East, XVII, pp. 285–6
2　Ibid, VI, p. 74
3　Quoted in *A Century of Our Sea Story* by Walter Jeffery (London 1900), p. 263
4　Travels in Southern Europe and the Levant 1810–1817. The Journal of C. R. Cockerell, R.A. (London 1903), ch. IV

5 *Companion Guide to the Greek Islands* by Ernle Bradford (London 1963), ch. 8

6 Herodotus, Bk VIII, cxi

7 *Memoirs of the Crusades. Villehardouin's Chronicle of the Fourth Crusade and the Conquest of Constantinople* trans. by Sir Frank Marzials (London 1957, Everyman), p. 30

8 *The Latins in the Levant*, p. 576

9 *Ibid*, p. 598

10 *A Voyage into the Levant* by Joseph Pitton de Tournefort, trans. from the French by John Ozell (London 1741, 3 vols), vol. II, Letter I

11 For some account of Creveliers (or Crevelier) see *Letters From the Aegean* by James Emerson (London 1829), vol. II, Letter xii

CHAPTER FIVE

1 Quoted in *The Latins in the Levant*, p. 596

2 Given in *Mykonos: Chronique d'une île de l'Egée* by Jean Baelen (Paris 1964), p. 35

3 Quoted from *La Grèce sanctuaire de la Méditerranée* by M. Christo Zalocosta in *Mykonos*, p. 39

4 *A Voyage into the Levant*, vol. II, Letter I

5 *The Cyclades*, ch. XI

6 *Odyssey*, XV, 412

7 *A Voyage into the Levant*, vol. II, Letter I

8 *Isles of the Aegean* by V. C. Scott O'Connor (London n.d.), ch. 3

9 *La Grèce Contemporaine* by Edmond About (5th edition, Paris 1863), ch. I, 1

CHAPTER SIX

1 *Odyssey*, XXII, 384–8

2 Memoirs of the Crusades. Joinville's Chronicle of the Crusade of St
   Louis trans. by Sir Frank Marzials (London 1957, Everyman), pp. 192, 175, 202

CHAPTER SEVEN

1 The Latins in the Levant, p. 608
2 Ibid, p. 618
3 See Essays on the Latin Orient by W. Miller (London 1921),
   pp. 175–7
4 The Cyclades, ch. XIV
5 A Voyage into the Levant, vol. I, Letter 5
6 Essays on the Latin Orient, pp. 400–1
7 Greek Memories by Compton Mackenzie (London 1939),
   pp. 427–9
8 Simiomata: A Greek Note Book, 1944–1945 by Richard Capell
   (London n.d.), ch. I

CHAPTER EIGHT

1 Isles of the Aegean, p. 225

CHAPTER NINE

1 The Shipwreck by William Falconer (London 1870), canto
   3, V
2 Letter to John Murray, Esq., on the Rev. W. L. Bowles's
   Strictures on the Life and Writings of Pope. February 7,
   1821
3 For some account of this episode see Dust upon the Sea by
   W. E. Benyon-Tinker (London 1947), chs. VIII, X, XIV

4   *A Voyage into the Levant*, vol. II, Letter 1
5   *The Cyclades*, ch. XVII

CHAPTER TEN

1   *Seriphos* by Phokion Galanos (Athens 1962. Text in Greek),
    p. 83
2   *The Latins in the Levant*, p. 597
3   *Seriphos*, p. 47
4   Ibid, p. 49

CHAPTER ELEVEN

1   Herodotus, Bk. III, 57–8
2   See *Siphnos* by A. G. Troullos (Athens 1961. Text in Greek),
    pp. 101–3
3   *The Cyclades*, ch. II
4   *Siphnos*, pp. 114–16

CHAPTER TWELVE

1   *Essays on the Latin Orient*, pp. 399–400

CHAPTER THIRTEEN

1   *The Latins in the Levant*, p. 625
2   *Mykonos*, p. 53
3   Quoted in *Mykonos*, p. 54, from *Voyage du Levant* by M.
    Robert (1714)

Index